American Language Hub

STARTER A
Student's Book

INGRID WISNIEWSKA
ED PRICE

macmillan education

Contents

Welcome

GREETINGS

0.1 **A** Read and listen to the conversation.

Jack: Hello! I'm Jack.
Alex: Hi. I'm Alex. Nice to meet you.
Jack: Nice to meet you, too.

B SPEAK Work in pairs. Practice the conversation. Say your name.

CLASSROOM INSTRUCTIONS

0.2 **A** Listen to the classroom instructions.

1 
Open your book

2 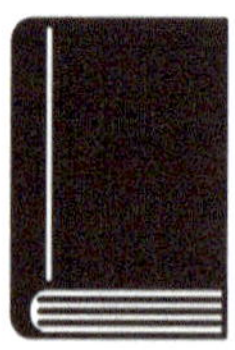
Close your book

3 
Read

4 
Listen

5 
Listen and repeat

6 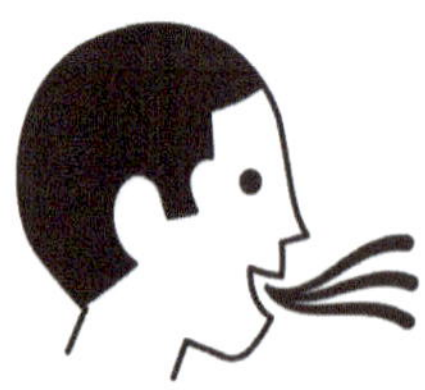
Speak

7 
Write

8 
Ask a question

0.3 **B** Read and listen to the conversations.

1 **Student:** What does *book* mean?
Teacher: It means *libro*.

2 **Student:** I don't understand.
Teacher: That's OK. I'll explain it again.

3 **Student:** Can you repeat that, please?
Teacher: Yes, of course.

THE ALPHABET

Aa Bb Cc Dd Ee
Ff Gg Hh Ii Jj Kk
Ll Mm Nn Oo Pp
Qq Rr Ss Tt Uu
Vv Ww Xx Yy Zz

***a*, *e*, *i*, *o*, and *u* are vowels.**
The other letters are consonants.

0.4 **A** Listen to the alphabet.

0.4 **B** Listen and repeat the alphabet.

0.5 **C** Listen and write the names.

1 ____________
2 ____________
3 ____________

D SPEAK Work in pairs. Spell your name.

A: Hello. My name's Lizzie. L – i – z – z – i – e.
B: Hi, Lizzie. My name's Florian. F – l – o – r – i – a – n.

1 NICE TO MEET YOU!

> The language of friendship is not words but meanings.
>
> Henry David Thoreau

A gondolier in Venice, Italy.

OBJECTIVES

- talk about where you're from
- introduce a friend
- greet people
- fill in a form

Work with a partner. Discuss the questions.

1 Look at the picture. Which country is the man in?
2 What language(s) do you think he speaks?
3 What language(s) do you speak?

1.1 Say hello

Talk about where you're from

V countries · P syllables and syllable stress · V numbers 0–10 · G simple present *be*: *I*, *you*

VOCABULARY
Countries

A SPEAK Work in pairs. Say hello. Say your name.

A: Hi, I'm Victor.
B: Hello, Victor. I'm Anna. Nice to meet you.
A: Hi Anna! Nice to meet you, too!

B Complete the greetings with names of countries.

Argentina Australia Brazil Britain Canada Egypt Italy Japan Mexico Morocco Spain ~~Turkey~~

Let's chat! It's easy! It's fun! Click and say hello!

1 Hi! I'm Emine. I'm from *Turkey*.

2 Hello, everyone! I'm Camilla. I'm from ______________.

3 Hello! I'm Alexa. I'm from ______________.

4 Hi, everyone! I'm Laura. I'm from ______________.

5 Hi! I'm Yasmin. I'm from ______________.

6 Hi, everyone! I'm David. I'm from ______________.

7 Hi! I'm Matteo. I'm from ______________.

8 Hello, I'm Emily. I'm from ______________!

9 Hello, everyone. I'm Hiro. I'm from ______________.

10 Hi! I'm Charlotte. I'm from ______________.

11 Hello! I'm Mark. I'm from ______________.

12 Hi, everyone. I'm Hamid. I'm from ______________.

C SPEAK Work in pairs. Ask about each picture.

A: Where is it? *B: It's in Egypt.*

A pyramid in Egypt

Mount Fuji

Sydney Opera House

The leaning tower of Pisa

PRONUNCIATION
Syllables and syllable stress

In English, we stress a different part of different words. A stressed syllable is loud and strong.

Ar-gen-ti-na

1.1 **A** Listen. Underline the stressed syllable in each word. Which word only has one syllable?

1 Argentina
2 Australia
3 Brazil
4 Canada
5 China
6 Egypt
7 Italy
8 Japan
9 Mexico
10 Morocco
11 Spain
12 Turkey

B SPEAK Work in pairs. Ask your partner about these cities. Then underline the stressed syllable.

1 Berlin, Germany
2 Budapest, Hungary
3 Bogotá, Colombia
4 Jakarta, Indonesia
5 Moscow, Russia
6 Stockholm, Sweden

A: Where's Berlin?
B: It's in Germany.

LISTENING

A PREDICT Look at the photo. Read the information. Where are they?

1.2 **B LISTEN FOR SPECIFIC INFORMATION** Listen to the conversation. Which city is the student from?

1.2 **C LISTEN FOR DETAIL** Listen again. Find and correct three mistakes in the form.

Application for Language School

First name:	*Luisa*
Last name:	*Fuentez*
Country:	*Italy*
Phone number:	*07647 293387*

D SPEAK Work in pairs. Ask and answer.

A: Where are you from?
B: I'm from Turkey.

VOCABULARY
Numbers 0–10

1.3 **A** Listen and repeat each number.

0 1 2 3 4 5
6 7 8 9 10

1.4 **B** Listen to Lisa's phone number. How does she say the numbers in bold?

07647 293387

1.5 **C** Listen and complete the phone numbers.

CONTACTS

1 01501 __77 2__9
2 767__ 022 14__4
3 0231 74__ 852__
4 073__ 630 433__

D SPEAK Work in a group. Ask each person for their phone number. Make a list.

A: What's your phone number?
B: It's 07790 521006.

GRAMMAR
Simple present *be: I, you*

1.6 **A** Listen to the examples. Underline the verbs.

I'm from Spain.
Are you from Madrid?
No, I'm not. I'm from Bilbao.

I am = I'm

B WORK IT OUT Circle the correct verb.

am/are		
I	[1]*'m / 're*	from Spain.
You	[2]*'m / 're*	from Turkey.
I	[3]*'m not / aren't*	from New York.
You	[4]*'m not / aren't*	from Toronto.
[5]*Am / Are* you from Brazil?		No, I [6]*'m not / aren't.*

C Go to the Grammar Hub on page VI.

SPEAKING

A PREPARE Read the conversation. Practice the conversation with a partner.

A: Hi! I'm Thomas. I'm from Argentina.
B: Nice to meet you, Thomas. I'm Anna. I'm from Germany.
A: Are you from Berlin?
B: No, I'm not. I'm from Hamburg.
A: Nice to meet you, too.

B PLAN Change the underlined words so the information is about you and your partner.

C PRACTICE Work in pairs. Practice your conversation.

D REPEAT Find a new partner. Practice the conversation again.

Talk about where you're from

1.2 What's your job?

Introduce a friend

V jobs **S** identifying personal pronouns **G** simple present *be: he, she, it* **P** contractions with *be*

VOCABULARY

Jobs

A SPEAK Work in pairs. Which jobs can you name?

B Match the words in the box with the pictures in Exercise A.

an architect a computer programmer a designer a doctor an engineer a manager a student a teacher

1.7 **C** Listen and check your answers.

D Go to the Vocabulary Hub on page XVIII.

READING

A READ FOR GIST Read the emails. What is Emma's job?

New job!
To: fashionista@mailhub.com
From: em173@design.nett

Hi Emma,
How's your new job? Is it fun? Is your manager nice? Please tell me all about it!
Keira

RE: New job!
To: em173@design.nett
From: fashionista@mailhub.com

Hi Keira,
Today is my first day in my new job!
I'm on the design team. It's a small team with five people. My manager isn't very friendly, but she's OK. Her name is Amanda and she's from Brazil.
My colleague Anton is nice. He's new today, too. I'm not very busy because it's my first day.
How are you?
Emma
P.S. Here's a photo of me in my new job as a designer.

B READ FOR DETAIL Read the emails again. Circle the correct answer.

1 *Keira* / *Emma* is in a new job.
2 She's on a *small* / *big* team.
3 Her manager *is* / *isn't* very friendly.
4 Her manager is from *Brazil* / *Canada*.
5 Anton *is* / *isn't* new.

Identifying personal pronouns

Pronouns talk about a noun.

My colleague Anton is nice. **He**'s new today too.

C READ FOR DETAILED UNDERSTANDING What do the words in bold refer to? Circle the noun.

1 How's your new job? Is **it** fun?
2 I'm on the design team. **It**'s a small team with five people.
3 My manager isn't very friendly, but **she**'s OK.
4 Her name is Amanda and **she**'s from Brazil.

GRAMMAR

Simple present *be: he, she, it*

A Read the examples from the emails. Underline the verbs.

It's a small team with five people.

My manager isn't very friendly, but she's OK.

My colleague Anton is nice.

How's your new job? Is it fun?

B **WORK IT OUT** Complete the table with *'s*, *is* or *isn't*.

Simple present *be: he, she, it*	
Positive	He/She/It ________ nice.
Negative	He/She/It ________ nice.
Question	________ he/she/it fun?

C Go to the Grammar Hub on page VI.

D Look at the verbs in the first two sentences in Exercise A. What are the full forms of these verbs?

It's a small team with five people. = It is a small team with five people.

E **SPEAK** Work in pairs. Ask questions about your classmates.

A: Is Anna from Italy?
B: Yes, she is. She's from Milan.
A: Is Raúl a doctor?
B: No, he isn't. He's an architect.

PRONUNCIATION

Contractions with *be*

1.8 **A** Read and listen to the examples. Listen to the pronunciation of *he's*, *she's* and *it's*.

1. He's from Canada.
2. She's from Brazil.
3. He's new today, too.
4. She's really nice.
5. It's my first day.

1.8 **B** Listen and repeat the examples in Exercise A.

1.9 **C** Listen and circle the word you hear.

1. *He's* / *She's* from Vietnam.
2. *It's* / *She's* from Egypt.
3. *He's* / *She's* an engineer.
4. *He's* / *She's* a doctor.
5. *He's* / *It's* OK.

D **SPEAK** Work in pairs. Take turns saying sentences using *he's*, *she's* and *it's*. Listen to your partner. Do they say *he's*, *she's* or *it's*?

SPEAKING HUB

A **PLAN** Student A – Stay on this page. Student B – Go to the Communication Hub on page XXI. Imagine the man in the picture below is your friend. Complete the information about him with your own ideas.

First name ____________

Last name ____________

Country ____________

City ____________

Job ____________

B **PREPARE** Prepare to introduce your friend to your partner. Practice by yourself.

This is a picture of my friend. His name is Ollie. He's from …
He's ________.

C **PRESENT** Work in pairs. Introduce your friend to your partner.

D **REPEAT** Change roles and listen to your partner's introduction.

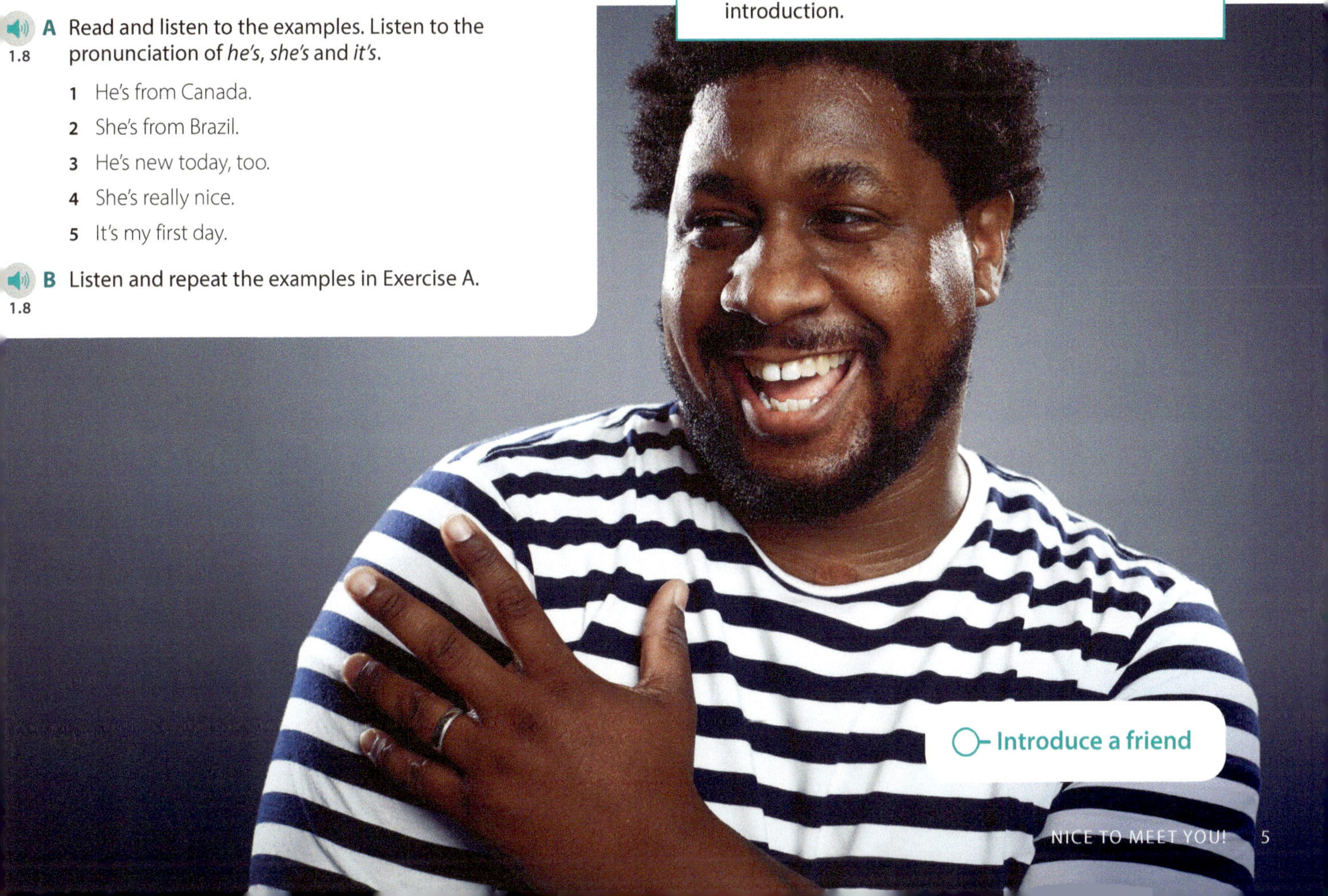

Introduce a friend

Café Hub

1.3 How are you?

F – greet people

COMPREHENSION

A Watch the video. Number the pictures (a–d) in the order you see them (1–4).

a ___ Sam's Café

b ___ Gaby's bedroom at night

c ___ The English School

d ___ Gaby's bedroom in the day

B Match the objects (1–8) with the places (a–d) in Exercise A. Then watch the video again and check your answers.

1 ___ books

2 ___ a mobile phone

3 ___ an alarm clock

4 ___ coffee

5 ___ a computer

6 ___ a credit card

7 ___ a calendar

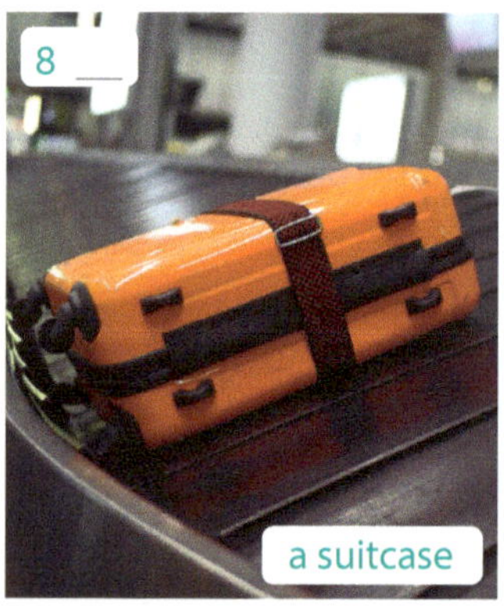
8 ___ a suitcase

C Match the numbers (1–5) with the letters (a–e) to make correct sentences.

1	Gaby is in	**a**	Gabriela García Martínez.
2	The café	**b**	is Sam's Café.
3	Gaby's coffee is	**c**	London.
4	Mark is	**d**	a cappuccino.
5	Gaby's full name is	**e**	Gaby's English teacher.

Glossary

mobile phone **(n) (British)** = cell phone **(n) (American)**

GABY

SAM

LUCY

D 01:32–02:28 Watch part of the video and correct the mistakes in the numbers on the form.

ENGLISH, ENGLISH, ENGLISH, AND ENGLISH

Student Registration Form

Name:	Gabriela García Martínez
Phone number:	00707 914865
Classroom number:	6
Teacher:	Mark
Time:	10 am

USEFUL PHRASES

00:40–01:28 Who says it? Sam (S), Gaby (G) or the receptionist (R)? Watch part of the video and check your answers.

1 Welcome to Sam's Café! ___
2 A cappuccino, please. ___
3 Thanks! ___
4 You're welcome! ___
5 Perfect! ___
6 Can I help you? ___

FUNCTIONAL LANGUAGE

Greeting people

A Complete the phrases in the table with the words in the box.

fine Hello morning See soon

Saying hello	Greeting people	Saying goodbye
1 ________ / Hi. Good 2 ________. Good afternoon. Good evening.	How are you? I'm 3 ________, thanks. And you?	Bye. See you 4 ________. 5 ________ you tomorrow.

B Watch the video again and check your answers to Exercise A.

PRONUNCIATION

A 1.10 Listen to the conversation. Notice how the underlined words are stressed.

Anna: Hello!
Stefani: Good morning. How are you?
Anna: Fine, thanks. And you?
Stefani: I'm fine, thanks. See you soon.
Anna: See you tomorrow.
Stefani: Bye!

B 1.10 Listen again and repeat the conversation. Copy the stress.

SPEAKING

A PREPARE Work in pairs. Practice the conversation in Pronunciation Exercise A again.

B PRACTICE Walk around the class. Greet your classmates.

A: Hi Onur. How are you?
B: I'm fine, thanks. And you?
A: I'm fine, thanks.
B: Great, see you soon.

Greet people

1 Writing

Fill in a form

W using capital letters

A Read the form. Where is Alex from? What is his job?

The Global Hub English School

Registration form

First name:	*Alex*
Last name:	*Johansson*
Home (city, country):	*Stockholm, Sweden*
Job:	*computer programmer*
Telephone number:	*451 3398765*
Email:	*ajohannsson@hub.com*

Email addresses

When we say email addresses, @ = *at* and . = *dot* (*ajohansson at hub dot com*).

B Read the form again. Check (✓) the words that need a capital letter.

- ☐ first names
- ☐ last names
- ☐ names of countries
- ☐ names of cities
- ☐ names of jobs
- ☐ email addresses

Using capital letters

We use capital letters for names of people and places.

WRITING

WRITE Complete the form with information about you.

The Global Hub English School

Registration form

First name: ______

Last name: ______

Home (city, country): ______

Job: ______

Telephone number: ______

Email: ______

Fill in a form

Unit 1 Review

GRAMMAR

A Complete the sentences with the positive (+) or negative (-) form of *be*. Use contractions if possible.

1 My name ___*'s*___ Jason. (+)
2 Carmen ___*isn't*___ from Greece. (-)
3 I ______ an artist. (+)
4 You ______ in my class. (-)
5 My manager ______ friendly. (+)
6 I ______ from Italy. (-)

B Write questions and answers in your notebook using the correct form of *be*.

1 you / from Paris (+)
Are you from Paris?
Yes, I am.
2 Leila / from Mexico (-)
3 you / a new student (+)
4 Tony / from Indonesia (-)
5 Anna / a student (+)
6 you / Japan (-)

VOCABULARY

A Reorder the letters to make the names of countries.

1 izrBal ______
2 yuTrek ______
3 pytgE ______
4 adanCa ______
5 tylaI ______
6 oMixec ______
7 nihaC ______
8 Sinap ______
9 apJan ______
10 natrAnige ______

B Complete the jobs with the missing letters.

1 d __ c __ or
2 computer p __ og __ __ m __ __ r
3 ar __ h __ __ e __ t
4 e __ __ i __ e __ r
5 fashion d __ __ i __ n e __
6 t __ __ c __ __ r

2 OUR MUSIC, OUR WORLD

Music is the universal language of mankind.

Henry Wadsworth Longfellow

Musicians playing in a mariachi band, Guanajuato, Mexico.

OBJECTIVES

- talk about nationalities
- ask for and give personal information
- ask for clarification
- write an online introduction

Work with a partner. Discuss the questions.

1 Look at the picture. What type of music is it?

2 Choose two words to describe the picture.

boring happy interesting
modern sad traditional

3 What do you think the quote means?

2.1 Where are they from?

Talk about nationalities

V languages and nationalities **P** syllable stress **G** simple present *be*: *we, you, they*; possessive adjectives

READING

A SCAN FOR INFORMATION Look at the pictures. Read the playlist. Where are the people from?

World Music fans!
Are you ready for some great new music?
On our playlist this week ...

Esperanza Spalding is a musician from Portland in the US. She's 33 years old and she's a jazz musician. Her songs are in English, **Spanish** and **Portuguese**. We're big fans of her new album!

Fatoumata Diawara is a singer and musician from **Mali**. She's 36 years old and a big star in Africa. Her album *Fatou* is one of our favorites, and our new favorite song is *Fenfo* from the new album *Fenfo (Something to Say)*!

Of Monsters and Men is a band of five people. They're from Reykjavík in Iceland. Their songs are really fun but they aren't in **Icelandic** – they're in English.

Monoswezi is an international band. Two of the band members are **Swedish**, one is **Norwegian**, one is from Mozambique and one is from Zimbabwe. Their music is a mix of African and European music. These musicians are super cool!

B READ FOR DETAIL Read the playlist and check (✓) the correct name.

	Esperanza Spalding	Fatoumata Diawara	Of Monsters and Men	Monoswezi
1 The people in this band are from one country.	☐	☐	☐	☐
2 Her songs are in three languages.	☐	☐	☐	☐
3 The people in this band are from different countries.	☐	☐	☐	☐
4 Their music is a mix of music from different countries.	☐	☐	☐	☐
5 This singer is from the US.	☐	☐	☐	☐
6 She's a big star in Africa.	☐	☐	☐	☐

C SPEAK Work in pairs. Which musicians in the playlist do you want to listen to?

VOCABULARY

Languages and nationalities

A Read the playlist again. Complete the languages and nationalities.

	Country	Language/Nationality
1	Spain	*Spanish*
2	Portugal	________
3	Iceland	________
4	Sweden	________
5	Norway	________

B Work in pairs. Write the nationalities of these musicians. Choose an ending from the box.

~~-ese~~ -ian -ish

1 Midori is from Japan. She's Japan*ese*________.
2 Marisa Monte is from Brazil. She's Brazil________.
3 Bono is from Ireland. He's Ir________.

C Go to the **Vocabulary Hub** on **page XVIII**.

PRONUNCIATION

Syllable stress

2.1 **A** Listen to the countries and nationalities. Underline the stressed syllables in the nationalities. Do the countries and nationalities have the same or different stress?

1 Sweden Swedish *same / different* (same circled)
2 Egypt Egyptian *same / different*
3 Iceland Icelandic *same / different*

2.1 **B** Listen again and repeat.

2.2 **C** Listen and underline the stressed syllable in each country and nationality. Is the stress the same or different?

1 China – Chinese *same / different* (different circled)
2 Turkey – Turkish *same / different*
3 Canada – Canadian *same / different*
4 Poland – Polish *same / different*
5 Italy – Italian *same / different*

2.2 **D** Listen again and repeat.

E SPEAK Work in pairs. Add another country and nationality for each ending.

	Country	Nationality
1	______	______ese
2	______	______ish
3	______	______(i)an

GRAMMAR

Simple present *be: we, you, they*

A Read the examples from the playlist. Underline the verbs.

Are you ready for some great new music?
They're from Reykjavík in Iceland.
… but they aren't in Icelandic – they're in English.
We're big fans of her new album.

B WORK IT OUT Complete the table with the positive and negative forms of the verb *be*.

Subject	Positive	Negative
I	'm / am	'm not
you	're / are	aren't
he/she/it	's / is	isn't
we	______	______
you	______	______
they	______	______

C Go to the Grammar Hub on page VIII.

D SPEAK Complete the questions. Then ask and answer them with your partner.

1 *Are / Is* you a fan of world music?
2 *Are / Is* your favorite musicians from America?

Possessive adjectives

A Read the examples. Underline the possessive adjectives.

On our playlist this week …
Their songs are really fun.
We're big fans of her new album!

B WORK IT OUT Complete the table with possessive adjectives from the box.

Her His Its ~~My~~ Our Their Your

Subject pronoun	Possessive adjective
I am a world music fan.	1 ___My___ name is Luciana.
You are from Brazil.	2 ______ songs are in Portuguese.
She is a singer from Mali.	3 ______ songs are sad.
He is from Sweden.	4 ______ songs are in Swedish.
This is the new album.	5 ______ name is *Fenfo*.
We are world music fans.	6 ______ playlist is cool.
They are from Iceland.	7 ______ music is full of energy.

C PRACTICE Circle the correct possessive adjective.

1 They're in a band. *Her / Their* new album is great.
2 We're fans of great music. *Our / Their* favorite music is from Brazil.
3 She's a musician. *His / Her* name is Ariane.
4 He's a singer. *Her / His* name is Michael.

D Go to the Grammar Hub on page VIII.

SPEAKING

A PREPARE Write information about your favorite musician or band.

Name: ______
Country: ______
Age: ______
Name of album or song: ______
______

B DISCUSS Work in pairs. Tell your partner about your favorite musician or band.

C REPORT Tell the class about your partner's favorite musician or band.

Talk about nationalities

2.2 When are you free?

Ask for and give personal information

V days of the week; numbers 11–100 S identifying context G *wh-* questions with *be* P contractions in questions

VOCABULARY

Days of the week

A Read the flyer. Which class looks fun?

INTERNATIONAL CENTER
ADULT EVENING CLASSES

Learn something new!
Learn about other cultures and meet people!
All classes start at 7 pm

MONDAY
Spanish guitar classes
60 mins Room 8

TUESDAY
African drums workshop
75 mins Room 24

WEDNESDAY
Arabic language class
90 mins Room 12

THURSDAY no classes

FRIDAY
Yoga for everyone
45 mins Room 18

SATURDAY AND SUNDAY no classes

2.3 **B** Listen and repeat the days of the week.

C SPEAK Work in pairs. Ask your partner questions about the classes.

A: What day is yoga?
B: Friday!

Numbers 11–100

2.4 **A** Listen and repeat the numbers. Notice the stressed syllable.

11 eleven	20 twenty
12 twelve	30 thirty
13 thirteen	40 forty
14 fourteen	50 fifty
15 fifteen	60 sixty
16 sixteen	70 seventy
17 seventeen	80 eighty
18 eighteen	90 ninety
19 nineteen	100 one hundred

B Go to the Vocabulary Hub on page XVIII.

2.5 **C** SPEAK Work in pairs. Circle all the numbers in the flyer and say them with your partner. Then listen and check.

LISTENING

2.6 **A** LISTEN FOR GIST Listen to three conversations. Write the number of the conversation.

Who are they?

a teachers ______
b students ______
c friends *Conversation 1*

1

2

3

Identifying context

Greetings such as *Good morning* or *Good afternoon* are more formal.

Hi! and *Hello!* are less formal.

2.6 **B** LISTEN FOR DETAIL Match the greetings in the box with the conversations (1–3).

Good afternoon! Hello! Hi!
Nice to meet you! (x2)

2.6 **C** LISTEN FOR DETAIL Listen again. Choose the correct answers to complete the sentences.

1 Kara's teacher is …
a Spanish. **b** Argentinian.

2 Maria and Angelo are in classroom …
a 12B. **b** 12C.

3 Maria and Angelo are in …
a a Spanish class. **b** an Arabic class.

4 Leila is …
a the Arabic teacher. **b** the yoga teacher.

GRAMMAR
Wh- questions with *be*

A Read the examples. Underline the question words.

What's your name? When are you free?
Who's your teacher? How old are you?
Where's she from?

B WORK IT OUT Choose the correct word to complete the questions.

1 **What / Who** are their jobs?
2 **When / How** old are Kara and Pete?
3 **What / Where** are they from?
4 **What / Who** is your teacher?
5 **When / What** is your Spanish class?

C WORK IT OUT Choose the correct options to complete the rules.

wh- questions with *be*

1 In *wh-* questions, the ***verb / question word*** is first.
2 In *wh-* questions, the ***verb / question word*** is second.

D Go to the Grammar Hub on page VIII.

E PRACTICE Complete the questions with the correct form of the verb *be*. Then match the questions (1–5) with the answers (a–e).

1 What __________ their names?
2 Where __________ she from?
3 When __________ your yoga classes?
4 How old __________ your children?
5 Who __________ your favorite musicians?

a 5 and 8
b Lucia and Stefan
c On Fridays
d Of Monsters and Men and Coldplay
e Australia

F SPEAK Work in pairs. Use the prompts to ask and answer the questions.

1 When / your (English) classes?
2 Who / your teacher?
3 Where / your teacher from?

PRONUNCIATION
Contractions in questions

2.7 **A** Read and listen to these questions. Notice how *who* and *how* are pronounced.

1 **Who's** your teacher? 3 **Who are** you?
2 **How's** your teacher? 4 **How are** you?

2.7 **B** Listen and repeat the examples in Exercise A.

2.8 **C** Listen and choose the correct answer to the questions you hear.

1 a He's Mr. Parker. b He's really nice.
2 a I'm a new student. b I'm fine, thank you.
3 a She's OK, thank you. b Her name's Anna.
4 a This is Pedro and this is Yuki. b They're great!

D SPEAK Work in pairs. Write four questions using *Who's*, *How's*, *Who are* and *How are*. Then ask your partner.

SPEAKING HUB

A PREPARE Work in pairs. Student A – Stay on this page. Student B – Go to the Communication Hub on page XXIII.

Read the information. What questions can you ask to find the missing information?

1 *What's his name?* 5 __________?
2 __________? 6 __________?
3 __________? 7 __________?
4 __________? 8 __________?

B PRACTICE Ask your partner your questions from Exercise A to complete the information about each person.

a

Name	1 __________
Country	Argentina
Age	2 __________
Job	Designer

b

Name	Tomoko Kogawa
Country	3 __________
Age	35
Job	4 __________

c

Name	5 __________
Country	India
Age	6 __________
Job	Engineer

d

Name	7 __________
Country	Turkey
Age	25
Job	8 __________

Ask for and give personal information

2.3 I'm late

F – ask for clarification

COMPREHENSION

A Watch the video. Number the pictures (a–h) in the order you see them (1–8).

a ___

b ___

c ___

d ___

e ___

f ___

g ___

h ___

B Complete the information in the table. Watch the video again and check your answers.

Name	Gaby	3 ___	4 ___	Onur	7 ___
Nationality	1 ___	English	5 ___	6 ___	Italian
Job	2 ___	English teacher	primary school teacher	student	8 ___

USEFUL PHRASES

A Who says it? Gaby (G), Mark (M) or Carolina (C)? Watch the video again and check your answers.

1 Please sit down. ___
2 Yes, that's it. ___
3 Nice to meet you. ___
4 Hi, guys. ___
5 Now it's your turn. ___
6 I'm late! ___

B Student A – Mime a phrase in Exercise A. Student B – Say the phrase. Then change roles.

GABY

SAM

LUCY

FUNCTIONAL LANGUAGE

Asking for clarification

A Complete the phrases with the verbs in the box.

mean say understand

1 Carolina: How do you [1] ____________ *primário* in English?
Mark: 'Primary', I think.

2 Marta: I'm a nurse.
Carolina: I'm sorry, I don't [2] ____________.

3 Onur: What does 'nurse' [3] ____________?
Mark: *Enfermeira*

B 02:01–02:50 Watch part of the video and check your answers to Exercise A.

C Reorder the words to make the phrases.

1 mean? / What / 'student' / does

____

2 you / say / in English? / How / do / *obrigado*

____

3 understand. / I'm sorry, / I / don't

____

PRONUNCIATION

2.9 **A** Listen to the conversation. Notice how the underlined words are stressed.

Angela: Good morning, everyone. My name's Angela. I'm your English teacher.

Roberto: I'm Roberto. I'm from Italy. How do you say *medico* in English?

Angela: 'Doctor'.

Roberto: Oh yes, that's it. I'm a doctor.

Monika: Hi. My name's Monika. I'm Polish and I'm an architect.

Roberto: I'm sorry, I don't understand. What does 'architect' mean?

2.9 **B** Listen again and repeat the conversation. Copy the stress.

SPEAKING

A PREPARE You are going to introduce yourself to a group. Think about what you want to say.

- name
- nationality
- job

B PRACTICE Work in groups. Imagine you are in a new class. Practice your conversation.

C PRESENT Perform your conversation for the rest of the class.

Glossary

primary school teacher (n) (British) = elementary school teacher (n) (American)

Ask for clarification

2 Writing

Write an online introduction

W using *and* to join sentences

A Read the title and introduction of the blog post. What do you think Tina writes about?

address age birthday country job name nationality phone number teacher's name

GLOBAL HUB LANGUAGE SCHOOL

Home Forum About Login Sign up

Say hello to your classmates.
Post your introductions on this page.

Posted by: Tina Gonzalez

Hi, everyone! My name's Tina and I'm from Mexico. I'm 28 years old and I'm a photographer. My English classes are on Tuesdays and Thursdays. My teacher is Mr. Sampson. He's from Ottawa in Canada. I'm a big fan of British music. My favorite bands are Coldplay and Arctic Monkeys. Their music is really cool!

Using *and* to join sentences

We use *and* to link ideas. *And* gives extra information.

I'm 28 years old *and* I'm a new student.

B Read Tina's self-introduction again. Answer the questions.

1 Where's Tina from? ______
2 How old is she? ______
3 What's her job? ______
4 Who's Mr. Sampson? ______
5 Who are her favorite bands? ______

WRITING

A PLAN Imagine you are at a new school. Complete the information.

What's your name?	
Where are you from?	
What's your job?	
When are your English classes?	
Who's your teacher?	
Who are your favorite musicians?	

B WRITE Write an introduction for your school web forum. Use Tina's introduction to help you. Use *and* to join sentences.

Write an online introduction

Unit 2 Review

GRAMMAR

A Choose the correct verb to complete the sentences.

1 We *am* / *is* / *are* from Morocco.
2 My friend *am* / *is* / *are* Portuguese.
3 *Am* / *Is* / *Are* you a fan of world music?
4 Their names *am* / *is* / *are* Paolo and Pawel.

B Write the questions for these answers.

1 He's a teacher. *What's his job?*
2 They're from Brazil. ______
3 Her name is Elise. ______
4 My class is on Thursday. ______
5 I'm 34 years old. ______
6 My teacher is Mr. Stevens. ______

C Circle the correct possessive adjectives.

1 She's from Brazil and *his* / *her* songs are in Portuguese.
2 We're from Iceland, but *our* / *their* songs are in English.
3 They're from Senegal and *our* / *their* music is traditional.
4 You're from Mexico, but *my* / *your* name is German.

VOCABULARY

A Write the nationalities for these countries.

1 Brazil *Brazilian*
2 Canada ______
3 Iceland ______
4 Turkey ______
5 Egypt ______
6 Poland ______
7 Japan ______
8 Argentina ______

B Complete the days of the week.

1 M _ _ d a y
2 T _ _ s d a y
3 W _ d _ _ _ d a y
4 T _ u _ _ d a y
5 F _ _ d a y
6 S _ t _ _ d a y
7 S _ _ d a y

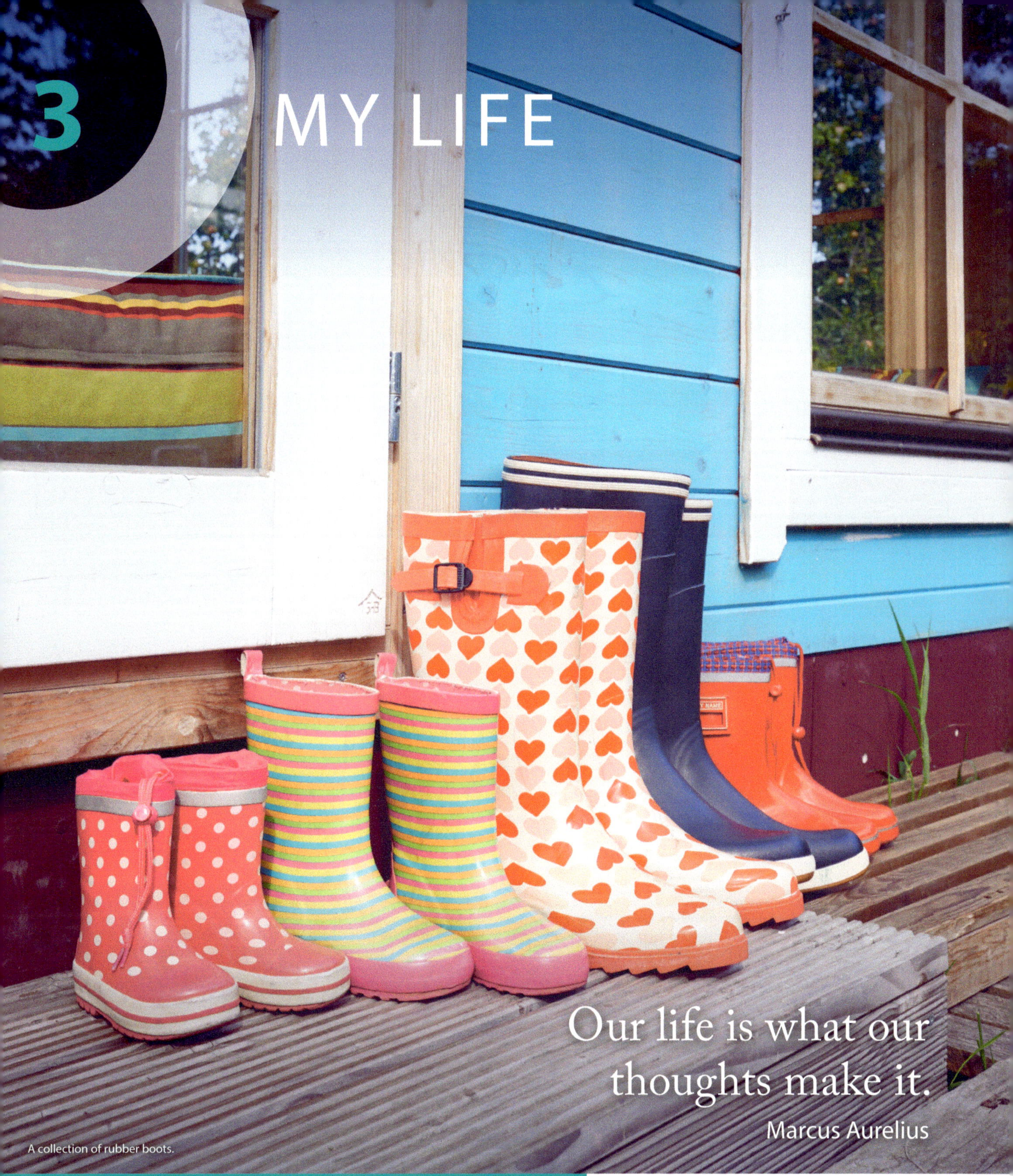

A collection of rubber boots.

OBJECTIVES

- describe everyday objects
- talk about your family
- describe people
- write a social media post

Work with a partner. Discuss the questions.

1 Choose words that match the picture.

family   home   job   nationality   school

2 Who do you think lives in the house?

3 Who is important in your life?

3.1 That's my coat

Describe everyday objects

V objects and colors G *a/an* and plural nouns; *this, that, these, those* P /s/, /z/ and /ɪz/

VOCABULARY
Objects and colors

A Look at the picture. Write the letter (or letters) for these words.

a hat ___
a phone ___
a sweatshirt ___
an umbrella ___
a bag *a*, ___, ___, ___
a coat ___, ___, ___, ___
glasses ___
headphones ___

B Look at the picture again. Write the correct letter.

Which coat is …

1 blue? ___ **3** green? ___
2 red? ___ **4** black? ___

C Go to the **Vocabulary Hub** on **page XIX**.

GRAMMAR
a/an and plural nouns

A **WORK IT OUT** Read the examples. Choose the correct options for the sentences in the box.

In the picture, …
letter j is a sweatshirt.
letter i is an umbrella.
letters k, l, m, and n are coats.

***a/an* and plural nouns**

1 We use *a/an* when there is ***one / more than one*** object.
2 We add *s* when there is ***one / more than one*** object.

B Go to the **Grammar Hub** on **page X**.

C **SPEAK** Work in pairs. Say the color and name of an object in the picture. Your partner says the correct letter.

A: A blue bag
B: Letter c!
A: Correct. White glasses …

PRONUNCIATION
/s/, /z/ and /ɪz/

3.1 **A** Listen and repeat the sounds and the words.

/s/ coats /z/ headphones /ɪz/ glasses

3.2 **B** Listen to the words. Choose the correct sound for the underlined letters.

1 umbrellas /s/ /z/ /ɪz/
2 hats /s/ /z/ /ɪz/
3 bags /s/ /z/ /ɪz/
4 classes /s/ /z/ /ɪz/

C **SPEAK** Work in pairs. Make a list of the objects from Vocabulary Exercise A that are in your classroom. Say how many.

A: an umbrella
B: sixteen black bags

LISTENING

3.3 **A** **LISTEN FOR GIST** Listen to the conversation. What is the problem?

3.3 **B** **LISTEN FOR KEY WORDS** Listen again. Look at the picture above and circle all the objects that you hear.

3.3 **C** **LISTEN FOR DETAIL** Listen again and answer the questions.

1 What's the woman's ticket number? ___
2 What color is the woman's coat? ___
3 What color are the woman's bags? ___ / ___

GRAMMAR

this, that, these, those

3.4 **A** Look at the pictures. Listen and complete the sentences from the conversation with *this, that, these* or *those*.

Coatroom attendant:	Is [1] _______________ your coat?
Customer:	No! My coat is blue. [2] _______________ coat is green.

Coatroom attendant:	Are [3] _______________ your bags?
Customer:	No! [4] _______________ bags are red and blue.

B **WORK IT OUT** Look at the pictures and sentences in Exercise A again. Match the numbers (1–4) with the letters (a–d) to complete the rules.

this, that, these, those

1 We use *this* and *that* to talk about …
2 We use *these* and *those* to talk about …
3 We use *this* and *these* to talk about …
4 We use *that* and *those* to talk about …

a more than one object.
b things that are not near.
c one object.
d things that are near.

C Go the **Grammar Hub** on **page X**.

D **PRACTICE** Write *this, that, these* or *those* and the name of the object for each picture.

1 _______________

2 _______________

3 _______________

4 _______________

SPEAKING

A **PRACTICE** Work in pairs. Practice the conversation.

Customer:	Can I have my hat, please?
Coatroom attendant:	Is this your hat?
Customer:	No. That hat is blue. My hat is green.
Coatroom attendant:	Is this your hat?
Customer:	Yes, that's my hat.

B **PREPARE** Work in groups. You are going to ask for your own objects at a coatroom.

One person is the coatroom attendant. Go to the **Communication Hub** on **page XXIV**.

The rest of the group are customers.

- Put some objects on the table. Try and put out more than one of the same type of object.
- Think about the names of the objects (hat, bag, headphones, etc).
- Think about the colors (red, blue, black, white, gray, brown, etc).
- Don't tell the attendant which object is yours.

Remember: *that/those*.

C **DISCUSS** Ask for your things at the coatroom. Use the conversation in Exercise A to help you.

D **REPEAT** Change roles and repeat.

A: Can I have my glasses, please?
B: Are these your glasses?
A: No, they aren't. Those glasses are brown. My glasses are black.

Describe everyday objects

3.2 I have two sisters

Talk about your family

S finding key information   V family   P schwa /ə/   G *have/has*

READING

A PREPARE TO READ Look at the picture. Choose three words from the box to describe it.

cake   family   job   party   restaurant

100 YEARS YOUNG!

Local woman celebrates her 100th birthday with her family.

Lilly Wenders is 100 years old this week, and there's a family party to celebrate. 'A lot of my family lives in the same town as me,' says Lilly. 'I'm very lucky.'

Lilly is not the oldest person in her family. She has two **sisters**. Agatha is 103 and Hattie is 106.

Lilly has two **children**, Sally and Emily, and three **grandchildren**: Katrina, Olivia and Clara. 'I don't have a **son** or a **grandson**,' says Lilly. 'My children and my grandchildren are all women.'

'Do you have any men in your family?' I ask Lilly.

'Yes, I do,' says Lilly. 'I have a **husband**, Arthur. It's his birthday this week, too, but he's only 84!'

Finding key information

Finding the important information first can help you to understand a text.

Examples of important information are:

- names (people, places)
- numbers (age, time, date)

B SCAN FOR INFORMATION Read the article quickly. Match the people (1–4) with their ages (a–d).

1 Lilly   a 84
2 Agatha   b 100
3 Hattie   c 103
4 Arthur   d 106

C READ FOR DETAIL Read the article again. Complete the statements with the underlined words in the article.

1 The party is for Lilly's ________.
2 Lilly lives in the same ________ as a lot of people in her family.
3 Lilly has a lot of ________ in her family.

D SPEAK Work in pairs. Answer the questions.

1 Do you know anyone who is 100 years old?
2 Do you live in the same town/city as your family?

VOCABULARY

Family

A Find the words in bold in the article. Put them in the correct place in the table.

Female	Male
mother	father
1 ________	brother
daughter	2 ________
grandmother	grandfather
granddaughter	3 ________
wife	4 ________
Female and/or male	
parents	
5 ________	6 ________

B Complete the family tree with names from the article.

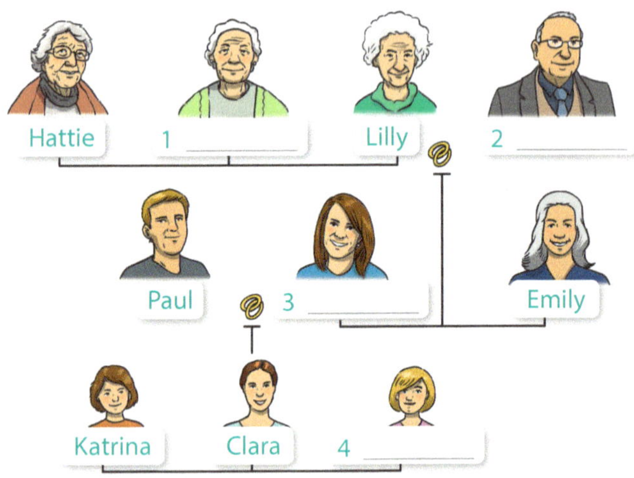

C Complete the sentences with words from Exercise A.

Arthur: 'Lilly is my ________.'

Hattie: 'Lilly is my ________.'

Emily: 'Lilly is my ________.'

Clara: 'Lilly is my ________.'

PRONUNCIATION

schwa /ə/

A Listen to the sentences. Notice how the underlined letters sound. 3.5

1 Lilly is my mother.
2 Arthur is my father.
3 Paul is my husband.
4 I have three children.

B Listen again and repeat. 3.5

C Underline the letters with the schwa sound. Listen and check. 3.6

1 daughter 2 parents 3 grandfather 4 brother

D Connect the words with the schwa sound to get out of the maze.

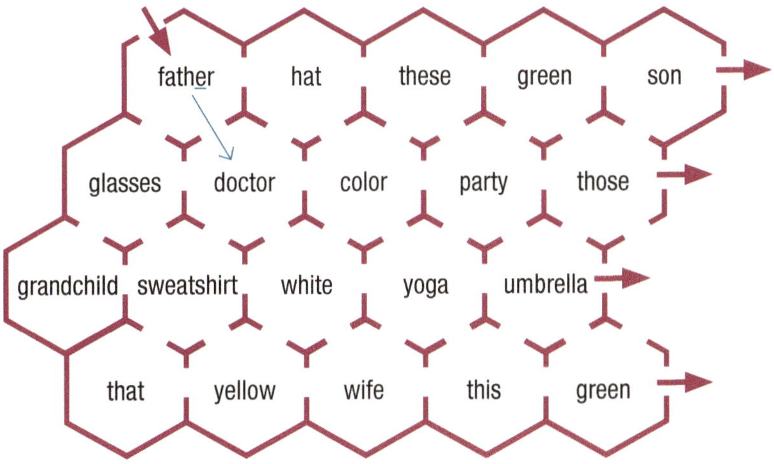

GRAMMAR

have/has

A WORK IT OUT Read the phrases from *100 years young!* Underline examples of *have/has*. Then choose the correct option to complete the rule.

Lilly has two children, …
'I don't have a son or a grandson, …'
'Do you have any men in your family?'
'Yes, I do, …' I have a husband, …'

have/has

We use *have/has* to talk about ***somebody's age / family members and things that we own.***

B WORK IT OUT Complete the table with the words in the box.

do doesn't doesn't have don't have has ~~have (x3)~~

have/has	
positive (+)	I [1] *have* a sister She [2] ______ a brother.
negative (–)	I [3] ______ a brother. He [4] ______ a granddaughter.
question	Do you [5] ______ a daughter? Does she [6] ______ a daughter?
answer	Yes, I [7] ______. / No, I don't. Yes, she does / No, he [8] ______.

C Go to the Grammar Hub on page X.

SPEAKING HUB

A PREPARE Draw your family tree on a piece of paper and write the family members. Don't write their names and don't write your name.

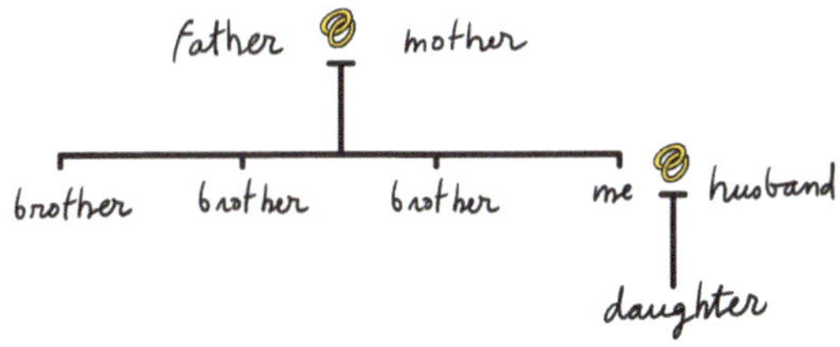

B DISCUSS Work in groups. Follow the instructions:

- Fold your family trees and put them in a box.
- Take out another person's family tree.
- Ask and answer questions. Find out who each family tree belongs to.

A: Do you have a sister, Nita?
B: No, I don't.
A: Do you have three brothers?
B: Yes, I do.
A: Is this your family tree?
B: Yes, it is!

C PRACTICE Ask each other more questions about the people in your families.

A: What's your brother's name?
B: His name's Hector.
A: How old is he?
B: He's 34.
A: What does he do?
B: He's a builder.

Talk about your family

Café Hub

3.3 Guess who

F– describe people

COMPREHENSION

A Watch the video. Number the events (a–d) in the order you see them (1–4). Is it easy for Gaby to meet Lucy?

a ___

b ___

c ___

d ___

B Are the sentences true (T) or false (F)? Watch the video again and check your answers.

1 Gaby sees Lucy's poster in Sam's Café. *T / F*
2 Gaby texts Lucy first. *T / F*
3 Lucy has a yellow jacket. *T / F*
4 Lucy is English. *T / F*
5 Lucy has a green scarf. *T / F*
6 At Sam's Café, all the women have green jackets. *T / F*
7 Gaby says she's not OK. *T / F*
8 Gaby is Lucy's new Spanish teacher. *T / F*

C Correct the false sentences in Exercise B.

D How many bags, chairs, etc can you see in the picture?

bags	*3*	laptops	___	men	___	tables	___
chairs	___	plants	___	people	___	women	___

GABY

SAM

LUCY

FUNCTIONAL LANGUAGE

Describing people

Subject + verb	Type	Color	Noun
I've got	long	brown	hair.
I have	light	brown	hair.
Gaby's got a		yellow	jacket.

A Put the words in 1–5 in the correct order. Use the box to help you.

1 got / a / jacket. / green / She's

____

2 got / They've all / jackets. / green

____

3 Lucy's / hair. / brown / light / got

____

4 got / Lucy's / bag. / black / a

____

5 gray / got / Lucy's / a / scarf.

____

B ▶ 01:39–02:20 Watch part of the video and check your answers to Exercise A.

C Complete the descriptions with the words in the box.

blond curly long straight

1 short _______________ hair

2 _______________ red hair

3 _______________ gray hair

4 _______________ black hair

D SPEAK Work in pairs. Play a game of *Guess who* in the class.

A: She has long brown hair.
B: Is it Sandra?
A: Yes it is.

PRONUNCIATION

3.7 **A** Listen to the conversation. Notice how the underlined words are stressed.

Jessica: Hi, Mark. Are you free at two o'clock?
Mark: Yes!
Jessica: Do you know Sam's Café?
Mark: Yes. See you there at two o'clock. I have light brown hair and a black coat.
Jessica: OK. I have long black hair, a green coat and a yellow scarf.

3.7 **B** Listen again and repeat the conversation. Copy the stress.

C SPEAK Work in pairs. Practice the conversation.

SPEAKING

A PLAN Work in pairs. You want to do a language exchange. Arrange to meet your partner – you don't know each other.

- Choose a time and a place to meet.
- Write notes about your appearance.

B PRACTICE Work in pairs. Write and practice a similar conversation to the one in Pronunciation Exercise A.

C REPEAT Swap roles. Choose a new time and place to meet.

Note

I've got (British) = I have (American)
She's got (British) = She has (American)

The word *got* is typically not used with *has* and *have* in standard American English.

Describe people

3 Writing

Write a social media post

W – using *but*

A Read the social media post. Whose birthday is it today? Match the picture with the event.

Florence Duprey
January 24, 9:21 am

Happy birthday to my sister Martina! Here we are at home. She's wearing the yellow sweater and has a big smile – she's one in this picture! Our mom took this photo. Today it's Martina's 30th birthday party! We have the cake, but Mom is late 😂! Our little sister Talia is here, too – she's in the yellow top next to her husband Larry. Martina has a husband, too. His name is Paulo – he's the one in the white sweater.

5 ♡ 20 9

Using *but*

We use *but* to join ideas that are different.
We have the cake, **but** *mom is late!*

B Read the post again. These sentences are all false. Correct the sentences.

1 Martina is two years old in the first picture.
______.
2 Martina's mom is at Martina's 30th birthday party.
______.
3 Martina has one sister.
______.
4 Larry is wearing a white sweater.
______.

WRITING

A PLAN You are going to write a social media post. Find a picture of people in your family on a special day. Plan what you want to say.

B WRITE Write a social media post for the picture.

Write a social media post

Unit 3 Review

GRAMMAR

A Complete the sentences with *this, that, these* or *those.*

1 ______ bag is red.
2 ______ bag is blue.

3 ______ bags are red.
4 ______ bags are blue.

B Complete the sentences with *is* or *are.*

1 This bag ___is___ green.
2 Those hats ______ yellow.
3 Those headphones ______ black.
4 These glasses ______ white.
5 This phone ______ gray.
6 Those bags ______ brown.

C Choose the correct option to complete the sentences.

1 *I have/ has* a son.
2 *Do you has / Do you have* a brown coat? Yes, I *do/does.*
3 I *don't have / doesn't have* a brother.
4 She *don't have / doesn't have* a granddaughter.
5 *Does / Do* he have a brother? No, he *don't / doesn't.*

VOCABULARY

A Complete the words for objects and colors.

1 My h e a d p h o n e s are g r e e n.
2 This u __ b ______ l __ is w ________.
3 I have a b ______ n s w ______ s h ______.
4 My g l ________ are g ______.
5 That is a b __ u __ c o __ t.
6 These are my __ l __ c k b __ g s.

B Use the information. Write the names of the people.

Angela is 6. Mary is 35. Cara is 70.

1 ___Cara___: 'Mary is my daughter.'
2 ______: 'Cara is my grandmother.'
3 ______: 'Angela is my daughter.'

Pietro is 10. Guillermo is 50. Giancarlo is 80.

4 ______: 'Pietro is my grandson.'
5 ______: 'Giancarlo is my father.'
6 ______: 'Guillermo is my father.'

4 TIME

Better three hours too soon than a minute too late.

William Shakespeare

Sunset over Alhambra Palace, Granada, Spain.

OBJECTIVES

- talk about daily routines
- talk about annual routines
- order in a café
- write an email about your routine

Work with a partner. Discuss the questions.

1 Look at the picture. Which words match the picture?

city countryside moon morning night ocean sky sun

2 What's your favorite time of day?

3 Read the quote. Are you usually early or late for things?

4.1 Every day

Talk about daily routines

V daily activities; time   G simple present: *I, you, we, they*   P sentence stress

VOCABULARY

Daily activities

A Match the sentences (1–4) with the pictures (a–d).

1 I finish work at six ten in the evening.
2 I get up at seven o'clock in the morning.
3 I go to work at eight thirty in the morning.
4 I get home at five o'clock in the afternoon.

B Go to the Vocabulary Hub on page XIX.

Time

C Complete the times with the numbers in the box. Then listen and check. (4.1)

eight	eleven	fifty	forty-five	nine	twelve

1

_______________ o'clock

2

_______________ ten

3

twelve _______________

4

_______________ thirty

5

_______________ fifteen

6

one _______________

LISTENING

A PREPARE TO LISTEN Read the information about the podcast. Then choose the correct options to complete the summary.

The title of this podcast series is *My life*. In this episode, [1]*three / two* people talk about [2]*the people they know / the things they do*. The people in this episode have the same [3]*hobby / job*.

B LISTEN FOR MAIN IDEA Listen to the podcast and choose the correct options to complete the sentences. (4.2)

1 Magne is Astrid's ...
  a brother. b husband.
2 Astrid and Magne live and work ...
  a in the same place. b in different places.
3 Astrid and Magne work ...
  a at the same time. b at different times.

C LISTEN FOR DETAIL Listen again. Circle the correct person: Astrid (A) or Magne (M). (4.2)

1	1 am go to bed	A / M
2	5 am get up	A / M
3	5:15 am start work	A / M
4	11 am get up	A / M
5	1:30 pm start work	A / M
6	1:30 pm finish work	A / M
7	8 pm go to bed	A / M
8	9:45 pm finish work	A / M

D DISCUSS Work in pairs. Which person's day do you prefer? Why?

GRAMMAR

Simple present: *I, you, we, they*

A Read the sentences from the podcast. Are they positive (+) or negative (–)?

a I get up at five o'clock in the morning. + / –

b I don't work in the morning. + / –

B **WORK IT OUT** Complete the table with the words in the box.

don't go go

Simple present: *I, you, we, they*			
subject pronoun	positive	subject pronoun	negative
I you we they	[1] ______ to work at eight o'clock in the morning.	I you we they	[2] ______ to work at six o'clock in the morning.

C **WORK IT OUT** Read the sentences again. Choose the correct option to complete the rules.

1 In positive sentences with *I, you, we,* and *they* we use *verb / do + verb*.

2 In negative sentences with *I, you, we,* and *they* we use *verb / don't + verb*.

D Go to the **Grammar Hub** on **page XII**.

E **PRACTICE** Complete the description with the correct positive or negative form of the verbs in the box.

finish get up (x2) go start ~~work~~

The night shift

I'm a doctor. For one week in each month, I [1] *don't work* during the day. I [2] ______ my job at ten o'clock in the evening and I [3] ______ at eight o'clock in the morning. I [4] ______ in the morning, like most people. I [5] ______ in the evening, and I [6] ______ to bed in the morning.

F **SPEAK** Work in pairs. What times do you think these people get up and go to bed?

5-year-old children | 80-year-old people
20-year-old people | People your age

PRONUNCIATION

Sentence stress

A (4.3) Listen and repeat the sentences. Which words are stressed – the red or the blue?

1 I go to bed at ten o'clock.

2 I don't go to bed at ten o'clock.

B (4.4) Underline the stressed words in the sentences. Then listen and check.

1 I read a book in the evening.

2 We don't watch TV in the morning.

3 They start work at eight o'clock in the morning.

4 They don't start at eight thirty.

5 I relax in the evening.

C (4.5) Listen and complete the sentences.

1 I ______ to ______ at ______ o'clock.

2 I ______ ______ in the ______.

3 They ______ ______ to ______ at ______ thirty.

4 We ______ ______ in the ______.

SPEAKING

A **PREPARE** Think about these daily activities. Check (✓) the ones that you do every day.

- ☐ get up
- ☐ have breakfast
- ☐ go to work/school
- ☐ start work/classes
- ☐ have lunch
- ☐ finish work/classes
- ☐ go home
- ☐ have dinner
- ☐ watch TV/a movie
- ☐ read a book
- ☐ talk to friends/family
- ☐ go to bed

B **PLAN** Write the times you do the things in Exercise A. Prepare how to say it.

C **DISCUSS** Work in pairs. Compare your daily routines. What's different? What's the same?

A: I get up at seven o'clock in the morning.
B: I get up at eight o'clock in the morning.

Talk about daily routines

4.2 Every year

Talk about annual routines

V months and seasons
G simple present questions: *I, you, we, they*
S using pictures before you read
P *do you* /dʒʊ/

VOCABULARY

Months and seasons

A Match the pictures with the seasons.

fall spring summer winter

B Listen and complete the calendar.

4.6

April August December July June March May November October September

January	*February*	______
______	______	______
______	______	______
______	______	______

C SPEAK Work in pairs. Answer the questions.

- Which season is it now?
- Which month is it now?
- Which season is your favorite?
- Which month is your birthday in?

READING

A PREDICT Work in pairs. Look at the pictures in the article *Nomads in Mongolia* but don't read the text. What do you know about these people's lives?

Using pictures before you read

Articles on websites and in magazines and newspapers usually have pictures. Look at the pictures before you read to get an idea of what the text is about.

B PREPARE TO READ Match the words in the box with the pictures (a–d) in *Nomads in Mongolia* opposite.

hills horse river tents

C READ FOR GIST Read the article. Match the correct question (a–d) with each paragraph (1–4).

a How often do they go to a different place?
b What are nomads?
c Where do they go in different seasons?
d Do they live in houses?

D READ FOR DETAIL Read the article again. Are the statements true (T) or false (F)?

1 Mongolia is in Europe. T / F
2 Nomads live in cities. T / F
3 Nomads live in a type of tent. T / F
4 Nomads have animals. T / F
5 In Mongolia, September is in the spring. T / F
6 Many nomads go to a river in the spring. T / F

E SPEAK Work in pairs. Answer the questions.

- Are there nomads in your country?
- Would you like to live in different places in your country at different times of the year?

NOMADS

in Mongolia

Mongolia is a large country in Asia, north of China and south of Russia. There's a lot of space, about 1.56 million km², but there aren't a lot of people. There are about 3,000,000 (three million) people in Mongolia and many of these people are nomads.

1 ___ Nomads are people who go to different places in different months or seasons. They don't live in cities, they live in the countryside.

2 ___ No, they don't. They don't have houses, but they have tents, called *gers*, and they have horses and other animals.

3 ___ Some nomads move thirty times a year, some move four times a year. Many nomads go to a different place in the spring and in the fall. In Mongolia, spring is March, April and May, and fall is September and October.

4 ___ In the spring, they go close to a river for water. In the fall, they go to the hills.

GRAMMAR

Simple present questions: *I, you, we, they*

A Read two of the questions from *Nomads in Mongolia*. Match the questions (a and b) with the correct question type (1 and 2).

a Where do they go? b Do they live in houses?

1 Question ___ is a *yes/no* question. The answer can be *yes* or *no*.

2 Question ___ is a *wh-* question. The answer depends on the question word.

B **WORK IT OUT** Read the questions again and find their answers in the text. Complete the rules.

Simple present questions: *I, you, we, they*

1 In *yes/no* questions we use *do* **before** / **after** *I, you, we,* and *they*.

2 In *wh-* questions we use a question word (for example *what, where, when* ...) **before** / **after** *do*.

3 To give short answers to *yes/no* questions we **use do or don't** / **repeat the main verb**.

C Go to the **Grammar Hub** on **page XII**.

D **PRACTICE** Reorder the words to make questions. Choose the correct question type.

1 go to work / you / when / in the morning / do

When do you go to work in the morning ?

a *yes/no* b (*wh-*)

2 you / go / to another country / in the summer / do

____?

a *yes/no* b *wh-*

3 talk to / in the evening / you / do / who

____?

a *yes/no* b *wh-*

4 in the same place / live / you / do / all year

____?

a *yes/no* b *wh-*

E **SPEAK** Work in pairs. Ask and answer the questions in Exercise D.

PRONUNCIATION

Do you /dʒʊ/

A 4.7 Read and listen to the questions. How does the speaker say the underlined words?

1 Do you live in the countryside?

2 When do you go to work?

B 4.8 Work in pairs. Say these questions. Then listen and repeat.

1 Do you get home at seven thirty?

2 Where do you live?

3 Do you read a book in the evening?

4 What do you do in the summer?

C **SPEAK** Work in pairs. Ask and answer the questions in Exercises A and B.

A: Do you live in the countryside?

B: No, I don't. I live in the city.

SPEAKING HUB

A **PREPARE** Work in pairs. Student A – Use the information below. Student B – Go to the **Communication Hub** on **page XXII**.

Student A – Write questions to find out information about the birds in the picture above.

1 what / called ____________________?

2 where / live ____________________?

3 where / go / August or September ____________________?

4 where / go / May or June ____________________?

5 how far / go *How far do they go every year* ?

B **DISCUSS** Ask your partner the questions in Exercise A. Complete the missing information.

C **DISCUSS** Read the information about gray whales. Answer your partner's questions.

Name: Gray whales

Where: Near Alaska and near Mexico.

When: In the fall (October, November, December) they go to Alaska. In the spring (February, March, April) they go to Mexico.

How far: About 10,000–12,000 miles per year (16,000–20,000 kilometers)

Talk about annual routines

Café Hub

4.3 Coffee chaos

F – order in a café

COMPREHENSION

A Watch the video without sound. Underline the correct word or phrase.

1. The first customer *is* / *isn't* sure what she wants.
2. Sam *is* / *isn't* sure what the customer wants.
3. The line *is* / *isn't* long behind her.
4. The other customers are *fast* / *slow*.
5. Sam *is* / *isn't* happy to see the customer again.

B Read the list of things you can buy in Sam's Café. Watch the video again. Check (✓) the things you hear.

coffee	☐	water	☐
latte	☐	soya milk	☐
cappuccino	☐	bread	☐
mocha	☐	croissants	☐
hot chocolate	☐	snacks	☐
tea	☐	soft drinks	☐

C Use a word from each column to describe the coffee the woman buys.

a small a medium a large	soya	cappuccino latte	to drink in to take away

D Who says it? Sam, the woman or the man in the line? Watch the video again and check your answers.

1. What type of coffee would you like? ____________
2. That's a great question! ____________
3. Come on! ____________
4. What kind of bread do you have? ____________
5. Medium! I mean medium. ____________
6. So, let me check. ____________
7. No problem. ____________
8. How big is a medium? ____________

E SPEAK Work in pairs. What do you think the phrase 'Come on!' means in this context?

Glossary

soya milk **(n) (British)** = soy milk **(n) (American)**

take away **(phrsal v) (British)** = take out or to go **(phrsal v) (American)**

GABY

SAM

LUCY

FUNCTIONAL LANGUAGE

Ordering in a café

A Complete the phrases with the words in the box. Then complete the headings with *Customer* or *Sam*.

Can check get have kind large One please Sorry want What you

A ________	B ________
What can I [1] ________ you?	[7] ________ I have a latte / a soya latte / a tea / a hot chocolate, please?
[2] ________ type of coffee would you like?	Do [8] ________ have soya milk?
Sure. Small, medium or [3] ________?	Can I [9] ________ a small, please?
So, let me [4] ________: you [5] ________ a medium soya latte to take away?	A soya latte, please.
[6] ________, we're closing now.	[10] ________ tea / hot chocolate, please.
	Two cappuccinos, [11] ________.
	What [12] ________ of bread do you have?

B Watch the video again and check your answers to Exercise A.

PRONUNCIATION

4.9 **A** Listen to the conversation. Notice how the underlined words are stressed.

Coffee seller: Good morning! What can I get you?
Customer: Can I have a coffee, please?
Coffee seller: What type of coffee would you like?
Customer: A cappuccino, please. Do you have soy milk?
Coffee seller: Sure. One soy cappuccino. Small, medium or large?
Customer: Can I have a medium, please? To go.
Coffee seller: So, you want a medium, soy cappuccino to go?
Customer: Yes, please.

4.9 **B** Listen again and repeat the conversation. Copy the stress.

C SPEAK Work in pairs. Practice the conversation.

SPEAKING

Coffee	small	medium	large
Latte	$2.00	$2.50	$3.00
Cappuccino	$2.00	$2.50	$3.00
Americano	$1.70	$2.20	$2.70
Mocha	$2.00	$2.50	$3.00
Hot chocolate	$2.00	$2.50	$3.00
Tea	$1.00	$1.50	$2.00

Croissant $2.00 Bread and jam $2.50

A PREPARE Work in pairs. Take turns being Student A and B. Replace the underlined words. Use the menu to help you.

Student A: What can I get you?
Student B: Can I have a cappuccino, please?
Student A: Small, medium or large?
Student B: Can I have a small, please?
Student A: Sure. One small cappuccino.
Student B: Thanks.

B PRACTICE Have a new conversation. Student A works in a café. Student B is a difficult customer. Practice your conversation.

C PRESENT Show your conversation to the class. Who is the best difficult customer?

Order in a café

4 Writing

Write an email about your routine

W – using contractions

A Read the email from Hadid to his friend Javier. Where does Hadid work?

To: Javier
From: Hadid
How are you?

Hi Javier,

How are you? I don't work in Madrid anymore. I work on an oil rig. It's in the middle of the ocean. I work here every spring. I get to the oil rig in March, and I go home in April.

We get up at six o'clock in the morning, and we start work at seven. We finish work at seven o'clock in the evening – it's a long day! I don't have time to read a book or watch TV in the evening. I eat, talk to my family on the phone and go to bed at nine o'clock.

What about you? Where are you now? What's your job?

See you,

Hadid

Using contractions

When we write to friends or family, we can use contractions:

I'm for *I am*

it's for *it is*.

B Read the email again. Match the activities (1–6) with the months and times (a–f).

1 get to the oil rig	a 7 am
2 go home	b 7 pm
3 get up	c March
4 start work	d April
5 finish work	e 9 pm
6 go to bed	f 6 am

C SPEAK Work in pairs. Answer the question.

Do you think Hadid's routine is good? Why/Why not?

WRITING

A PLAN You are going to write an email to an old friend. Write notes about your daily routine.

B WRITE Write your email. Tell them about your daily routine. Use contractions.

Write an email about your routine

Unit 4 Review

GRAMMAR

Put the words in the correct order to make sentences.

1 do / get up / you / what time
What time do you get up ?

2 live / in Spain / they
________.

3 watch / TV in the evening / you / don't
________.

4 like / soccer / don't / we
________.

5 you / start work / when / do
________?

6 they / do / why / at five o'clock / get up
________?

VOCABULARY

A Complete the sentences with the words in the box.

get get up go (x2) finish watch

1 I ________ at six o'clock in the morning.
2 I ________ to work at eight thirty in the morning.
3 I ________ work at five thirty in the afternoon.
4 I ________ home at six ten.
5 I relax and ________ TV at seven thirty in the evening.
6 I ________ to bed at ten forty-five at night.

B Match the sentences in Exercise A with these times.

a 5:30 pm ___	c 6:10 pm ___	e 8:30 am ___
b 6 am ___	d 10:45 pm ___	f 7:30 pm ___

C Complete the words in these sentences.

1 My birthday is in F _ _ _ _ _ _ _.
2 My favorite season is _ _ _ t _ _.
3 _ _ _ is the month after April.
4 In my country, the _ _ m _ _ _ is June, July and A _ _ _ _ _.

5 TIME FOR A BREAK

Guard well your spare moments.

Ralph Waldo Emerson

Two men sitting on metal drums, Perth, Australia.

OBJECTIVES

- talk about free time
- talk about food and meals
- ask for information
- write a blog about food

Work with a partner. Discuss the questions.

1 Look at the picture. Why are these people happy?

2 What's your favorite food?

3 What makes you feel happy?

5.1 Relax and be happy

Talk about free time

V free-time activities G simple present: *he, she, it* P *does he / does she*

VOCABULARY

Free-time activities

A Look at the pictures. What is the same about all these activities?

1 
______ for a walk

2 
______ in the backyard

3 
______ a meal

4 
______ a bath

5 
______ shopping

6 
______ chess

7 
______ to the gym

8 
______ running

5.1 **B** Match the verbs with the pictures. Listen and check.

cook go (x4) take play sit

C SPEAK Work in pairs. What do you do to relax?

LISTENING

5.2 **A LISTEN FOR GIST** Listen to an interview. Which of the free-time activities from Vocabulary Exercise A do the people talk about?

5.2 **B LISTEN FOR DETAIL** Listen again. Are these sentences true (T) or false (F)?

1 The man eats lunch in his office. *T / F*
2 The woman goes to the gym on her lunch break. *T / F*
3 The woman goes for a walk after work. *T / F*
4 The woman watches TV in the evening. *T / F*
5 The man goes running after work. *T / F*
6 The woman goes running on the weekend. *T / F*

GRAMMAR

Simple present: *he, she, it*

A Read the examples. Underline the verbs.

He works all the time! He doesn't even take coffee breaks.

Does she go to the gym every day?

No, she doesn't. She goes about twice a week.

She doesn't have time to relax!

B **WORK IT OUT** Complete the rules with words in the box.

does   doesn't   main verb   question word   without

Simple present: *he, she, it*

1. In positive sentences, we use the ________________ plus *-s* or *-es*.
2. In negative sentences, we use ________________ plus the main verb without *-s*.
3. In *yes/no* questions, we use *Does* followed by the subject and the main verb ________________ *-s*.
4. In short answers, we use ________________ or *doesn't*.
5. In *wh-* questions, we use a ________________ and *does* plus the main verb without *-s*.

C **PRACTICE** Choose the correct option to complete the sentences.

1. Martin *cook* / *cooks* dinner in the evening.
2. Anna *don't* / *doesn't* go shopping after work.
3. Does Paolo *play* / *plays* chess?
4. What does Shyama *do* / *does* on the weekend?
5. **A:** Does Akira *takes* / *take* a bath after work?
   B: Yes, he *takes* / *does*.

D Go to the **Grammar Hub** on **page XIV**.

E **PRACTICE** Complete the conversation.

Anna: What do you [1]________________ to relax on the weekend? Do you go shopping?

Bea: No, I don't. My husband [2]________________ shopping, and I [3]________________ running. What about you?

Anna: I [4]________________ to the gym and my husband [5]________________ TV and [6]________________ computer games.

Bea: That sounds good. What kind of games [7]________________ he play?

Anna: He [8]________________ action games.

PRONUNCIATION

does he / does she

A Read and listen to the questions. Notice how the speaker links the underlined words together.
5.3

1. Does he go the gym?
2. Does she go running?

B Listen to each question and circle the words you hear.
5.4

1. *Does he* / *Does she* cook dinner every night?
2. *Does he* / *Does she* go shopping on the weekend?
3. What *does he* / *does she* do at lunchtime?
4. What kind of food *does he* / *does she* cook?

C Listen and repeat the questions in Exercise B.
5.4

SPEAKING

A **PREPARE** Complete the table with your free-time activities. Write three activities in each box.

	Me	My partner
On your lunch break		
In the evening		
On the weekend		

B **DISCUSS** Work in pairs. Ask your partner questions to complete the table. How many things are the same for both of you?

What do you do on your lunch break? Do you go for a walk?

C **REPORT** Tell the class about your partner.

Anton goes shopping on the weekend. He doesn't cook meals at home.

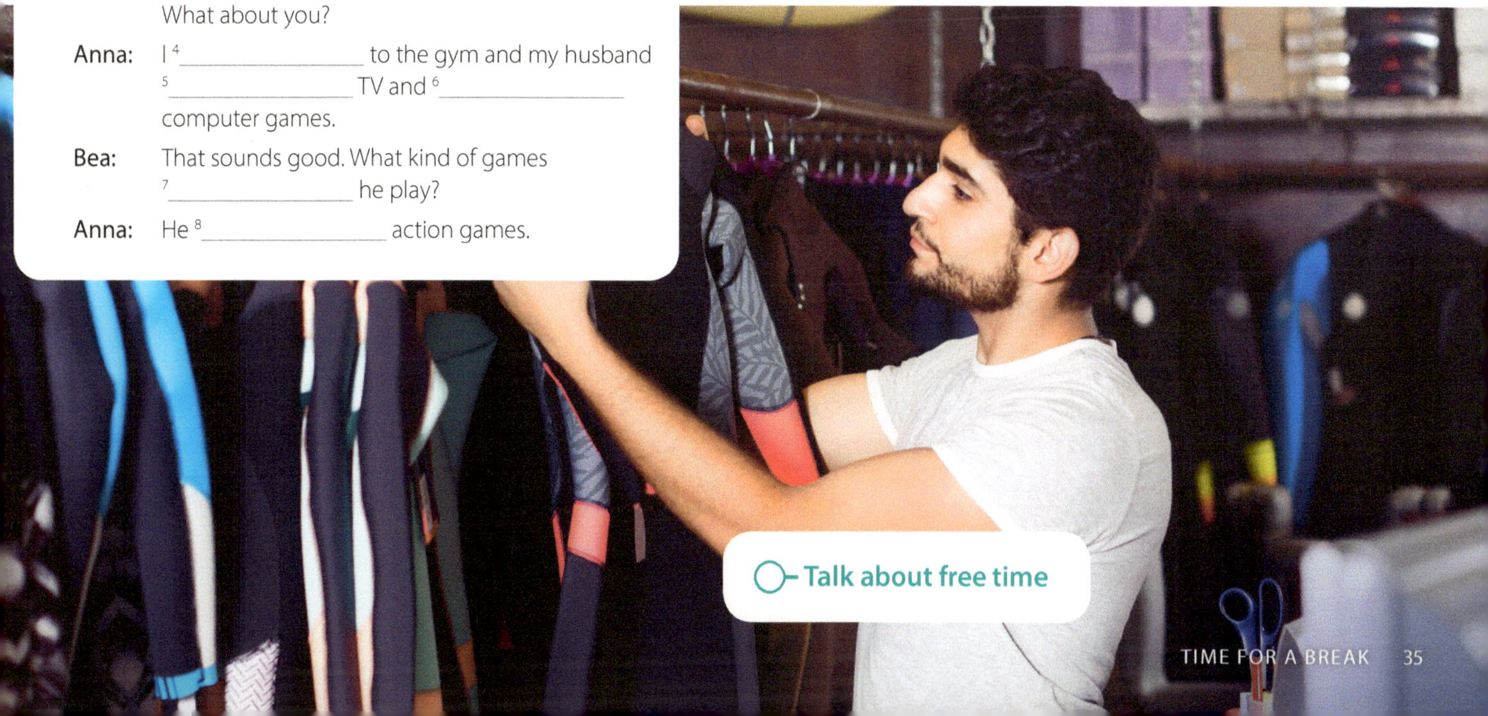

Talk about free time

5.2 When's your lunch break?

Talk about food and meals

V food and meals S skimming G adverbs of frequency P linking with /j/

VOCABULARY

Food and meals

A Look at the pictures. Which food do you eat for breakfast, lunch or dinner?

a  ____________
g  ____________
b  ____________
h  ____________
c  ____________
i  ____________
d 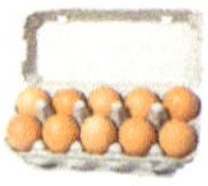 ____________
j  ____________
e  ____________
k  ____________
f  ____________
l  ____________

B Match the words in the box to the pictures.

apples beans bread cereal cheese chicken eggs fish noodles pasta potatoes rice

C Go to the Vocabulary Hub on page XX.

D **SPEAK** Make a list of food you eat every day. Tell your partner. What's the same? What's different?

READING

A **PREPARE** Work in pairs. Look at the pictures. Which foods can you name? Where do you think they come from?

 ____________
 ____________
 ____________

Skimming

When you skim a text, you read it quickly to get the general idea.

B **SKIM** Read *Lunch breaks around the world* and match the correct people with the pictures in Exercise A.

C **READ FOR GIST** Read the article. Which questions do all three people answer? Check (✓) the questions.

a What do you eat for lunch? ☐
b Is your lunch expensive? ☐
c What time is your lunch break? ☐
d Who do you eat lunch with? ☐
e Where do you eat lunch? ☐
f Do you eat a big lunch? ☐

D **READ FOR DETAIL** Read the article again. Write the correct names.

1 ____________ eats soup for lunch.
2 ____________ doesn't eat rice for lunch.
3 ____________ eats lunch at work.
4 ____________ doesn't talk about a drink.
5 ____________ has lunch with family.
6 ____________ has more than an hour for lunch.

LUNCH BREAKS AROUND THE WORLD

More and more people in the US don't take a lunch break. They eat lunch at their desk instead. Here we take a look at countries around the world and what workers do on their lunch breaks.

Sara, Japan

We always take our lunch break at the same time every day, from 12 to 1. Some people bring a lunchbox from home, but I always go to the office cafeteria to eat with my colleagues. The food is usually really good. I usually have rice with fish or chicken and some vegetables. After lunch, I have a cup of green tea. I drink a lot of green tea every day because it's good for my health.

Davide, Italy

Our lunch break is from 1:30 to 2:30. Sometimes we go to a local restaurant for lunch, but I usually go home. My wife always comes home for lunch, and we eat together. We usually have a small dish of pasta. After that we have some freshly cooked meat or fish. My favorite is chicken in tomato sauce. For dessert, we always have some fruit and finally a cup of coffee.

GRAMMAR
Adverbs of frequency

A Find and complete the sentences with adverbs from *Lunch breaks around the world*.

1 The food is ________________ really good.
2 I ________________ have rice with fish or chicken and some vegetables.
3 ________________ we go to a local restaurant for lunch.
4 My wife ________________ comes home for lunch.
5 I ________________ have dessert.
6 I ________________ have some fruit or something sweet as a special treat.

B Complete the chart with *sometimes*, *usually* and *never*.

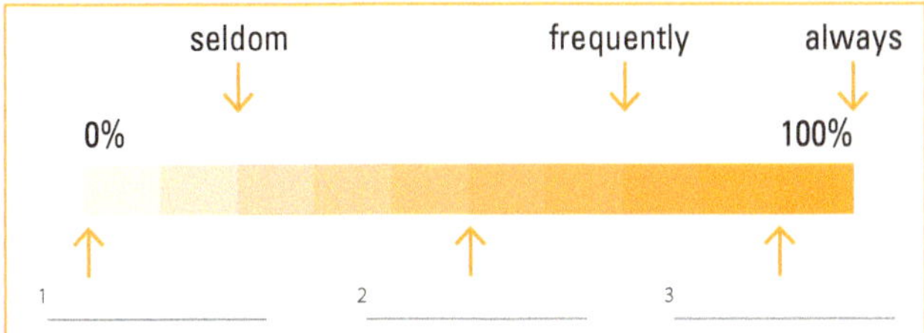

C WORK IT OUT Read the sentences in Exercise A and choose the correct option to complete the rules.

Adverbs of frequency

We use adverbs of frequency to say how often we do things. We put them …

1 *before* / *after* the verb *be* (in positive and negative sentences).
2 *before* / *after* other verbs (in positive sentences).

D Go to the Grammar Hub on page XIV.

E SPEAK Work in pairs. How often do you eat these kinds of food? When do you eat them? Tell your partner.

bread cheese chocolate coffee fish fruit ice cream milk rice tea

A: I usually have coffee for breakfast.
B: I frequently have coffee, but I sometimes have tea.

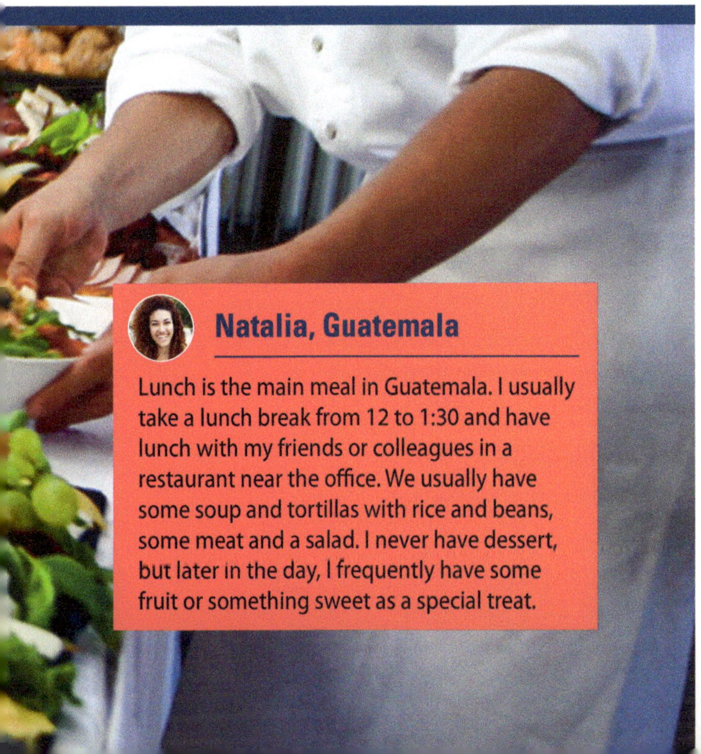

Natalia, Guatemala

Lunch is the main meal in Guatemala. I usually take a lunch break from 12 to 1:30 and have lunch with my friends or colleagues in a restaurant near the office. We usually have some soup and tortillas with rice and beans, some meat and a salad. I never have dessert, but later in the day, I frequently have some fruit or something sweet as a special treat.

PRONUNCIATION
Linking with /j/

5.5 **A** Listen to the sentence. Notice how the /j/ sound links the words joined with a ‿.

She‿always eats lunch at work.

5.6 **B** Read and listen. Draw a ‿ to show the words linked with a /j/ sound.

1 He always drinks coffee.
2 I usually have a salad.
3 She eats pasta for lunch.
4 We all eat fish and rice.

5.6 **C** Listen again and repeat the examples.

SPEAKING HUB

A PREPARE You are going to take a survey of eating habits in your class. Complete the questions (1–6).

EATING HABITS SURVEY

1 Do you *usually drink coffee for breakfast*?
a ____________ usually drinks coffee for breakfast.
2 Do you ________________________?
b ____________ always cooks dinner at home.
3 Do you ________________________?
c ____________ frequently eats lunch at work.
4 Do you ________________________?
d ____________ sometimes eats pizza for lunch.
5 Do you ________________________?
e ____________ never eats chocolate.
6 Do you ________________________?
f ____________ seldom eats meat.

B PRACTICE Ask your classmates the survey questions. Write names in sentences a–f. Ask each person another question to get more information.

A: Do you usually drink coffee for breakfast?
B: No, I don't.
A: What do you usually drink for breakfast?
B: I usually drink tea or hot chocolate.

C REPORT Tell the class about your answers.

Jerome doesn't drink coffee for breakfast. He usually drinks tea or hot chocolate.

Talk about food and meals

Café Hub

5.3 No battery

F – ask for information

COMPREHENSION

A Watch the video. Complete the information about the train ticket.

2 3 85 afternoon return

1 Gaby wants a ticket to Manchester on Saturday ________.
2 It leaves at ________ pm.
3 It takes about ________ hours.
4 She wants a ________ ticket.
5 It costs £ ________.

B Watch the video again and put the events (a–f) in the correct order (1–6).

a ___

b ___
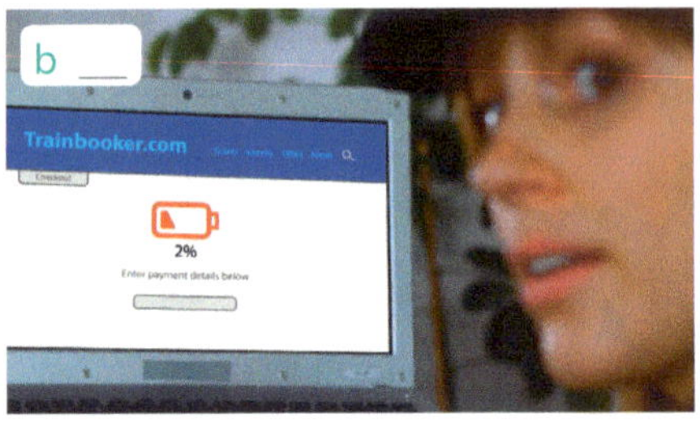

c ___

d 1

e ___

f ___

C Match the phrases (1–6) with the pictures (a–f) in Exercise B. Then watch the video again and check your answers.

1 It worked! ___
2 Gaby hates computers. d
3 Lucy needs Gaby's credit card. ___
4 There's no battery. ___
5 Lucy has an idea. ___
6 The wi-fi stops working. ___

USEFUL PHRASES

A Complete the useful phrases with the words in the box.

expensive idea matter news see worked

1 I have an ________!
2 Let me ________.
3 Good ________!
4 What's the ________?
5 Wow, that's ________!
6 It ________!

B Watch the video again and check your answers to Exercise A.

C **SPEAK** Work in pairs. Complete the conversations with useful phrases from Exercise A. Practice the conversations.

1 A: I don't have a ticket.
B: ________ – I have a ticket for you!

2 A: It's $150.
B: ________!

3 A: What time does it leave?
B: ________.

4 A: Oh no!
B: ________?

5 A: I don't know what to do!
B: ________!

6 A The code doesn't work.
B: Here – try this number.
A: ________!

GABY

SAM

LUCY

FUNCTIONAL LANGUAGE

Asking for information

A Write *Customer* or *Ticket seller* in the correct column, A or B.

A ____________	B ____________
1 I'd like a ticket to New York on Saturday afternoon.	a That's $85, please.
2 What time does it leave?	b It takes about two hours.
3 How long does it take?	c Saturday afternoon. Yes, there is a train.
4 Can I book a ticket please?	d One-way or round-trip?
5 Round-trip, please.	e It leaves at 3 pm.

B Match the phrases (1–5) with the responses (a–e).

Glossary

pounds (n) (British) = dollars (n) (American)
return ticket (n) (British) = round-trip ticket (n) (American)
single ticket (n) (British) = one-way ticket (n) (American)

PRONUNCIATION

5.7 **A** Listen to the conversation and notice how the underlined words are stressed.

Ticket seller: Can I help you?
Customer: Yes, I'd like a ticket to Boston on Friday morning, please.
Ticket seller: Friday morning. Let me see. Yes, there is a train.
Customer: What time does it leave?
Ticket seller: It leaves at 10:30.
Customer: How long does it take?
Ticket seller: It takes about three hours.
Customer: How much is it?
Ticket seller: Thirty-five dollars.
Customer: Can I book a ticket, please?
Ticket seller: One-way or round-trip?
Customer: One-way, please.

5.7 **B** Listen again and repeat the conversation. Copy the stress.

SPEAKING

DESTINATION	DEPARTURE	ARRIVAL	PRICE	
			one-way	round-trip
Washington, D.C.	10:30	12:30	$30	$55
Baltimore	10:45	11:45	$20	$30
New York City	11:00	1:30	$45	$60
Boston	11:15	3:00	$55	$80

A PREPARE Work in pairs. Complete the conversation using information in the timetable.

I'd like a ticket to ____________, please.
There is a train to ____________ this morning.
What time ____________?
It leaves at ____________.
How long ____________?
It takes ____________.
How much ____________?
One-way or ____________?
____________, please.
That's $____________, please.

B PLAN Work in pairs. Add three or more useful phrases to the conversation.

C PRACTICE Work in pairs. Practice the conversation.

D REPEAT Change roles. Choose a new destination.

Ask for information

5 Writing

Write a blog about food

W using object pronouns

A Read Bob's blog. What is the blog post about?

a	an everyday lunch	**c**	how to cook lunch
b	a special lunch	**d**	Bob's favorite lunch

BOB'S DAILY BLOG

A pot-luck lunch at work

Once a month at work, we have a pot-luck lunch. Everyone cooks some food at home and we bring it to the large meeting room. Some of my colleagues are really good cooks! They bring all kinds of food from their home countries. One of my colleagues is from Mexico and she makes a great chicken dish with chocolate. It's amazing!

I'm not a good cook and I usually just bring a salad. We eat and share all the food together – it's a great way to make friends at work!

B Read Bob's blog again. Are these statements true (T) or false (F)?

1. They have a pot-luck lunch every week. *T / F*
2. They eat the pot-luck lunch in a restaurant. *T / F*
3. A colleague makes delicious Mexican food. *T / F*
4. Bob is very good at cooking. *T / F*
5. Bob always brings cupcakes or cookies. *T / F*

Using object pronouns

We use pronouns so we don't need to repeat the noun.

Everyone cooks some ***food*** *at home and we bring* ***it*** *to the large meeting room.*

C Complete the sentences with the correct pronoun.

1. **My brother** works near my office. I meet ____________ for lunch every week.
2. We bring different **dishes** to work and share ____________ with each other.
3. **My sister** works in Mexico. I visit ____________ there every year.
4. I don't go out for **lunch**. I eat ____________ at my desk.

WRITING

A PREPARE You are going to write a blog about a special meal tradition in your life. Think about the following points.

- What's special about the meal?
- How often do you have it?
- Where is it?
- What kind of food do you have?
- What's good about this meal?

B WRITE Write your blog.

C REVIEW Read another person's blog. Ask questions to get more information.

Write a blog about food

Unit 5 Review

GRAMMAR

A Choose the correct words to complete the sentences.

1. Sasha ***sit / sits*** in the backyard after work.
2. Eric ***doesn't cook / cook*** dinner during the week.
3. Where does Maria ***eat / eats*** lunch?
4. Does Maha ***have / has*** lunch at school?
5. **A:** ***Do / Does*** Antonio and Sofia eat at home on Friday?
   B: No, they ***doesn't / don't***.
6. **A:** Does Jana ***drink / drinks*** tea every day?
   B: Yes, she ***do / does***.

B Add the adverb to each sentence.

1. I am ^never late for work. (never)
2. We eat breakfast in a café. (sometimes)
3. I cook dinner at home. (frequently)
4. Vicky and Sue have pizza on Friday. (usually)
5. Carey is very busy on the weekend. (always)

VOCABULARY

A Complete the phrases to describe recreational activities.

1	go for a w __ l __	**4**	go r __ __ __ __ __ g
2	take a b __ t __	**5**	go to the g __ m
3	cook a m __ __ l	**6**	play c __ e __ __

B Label the pictures with the correct words.

a

____

b

____

c

____

d

____

e

____

f

____

6 A PLACE TO LIVE

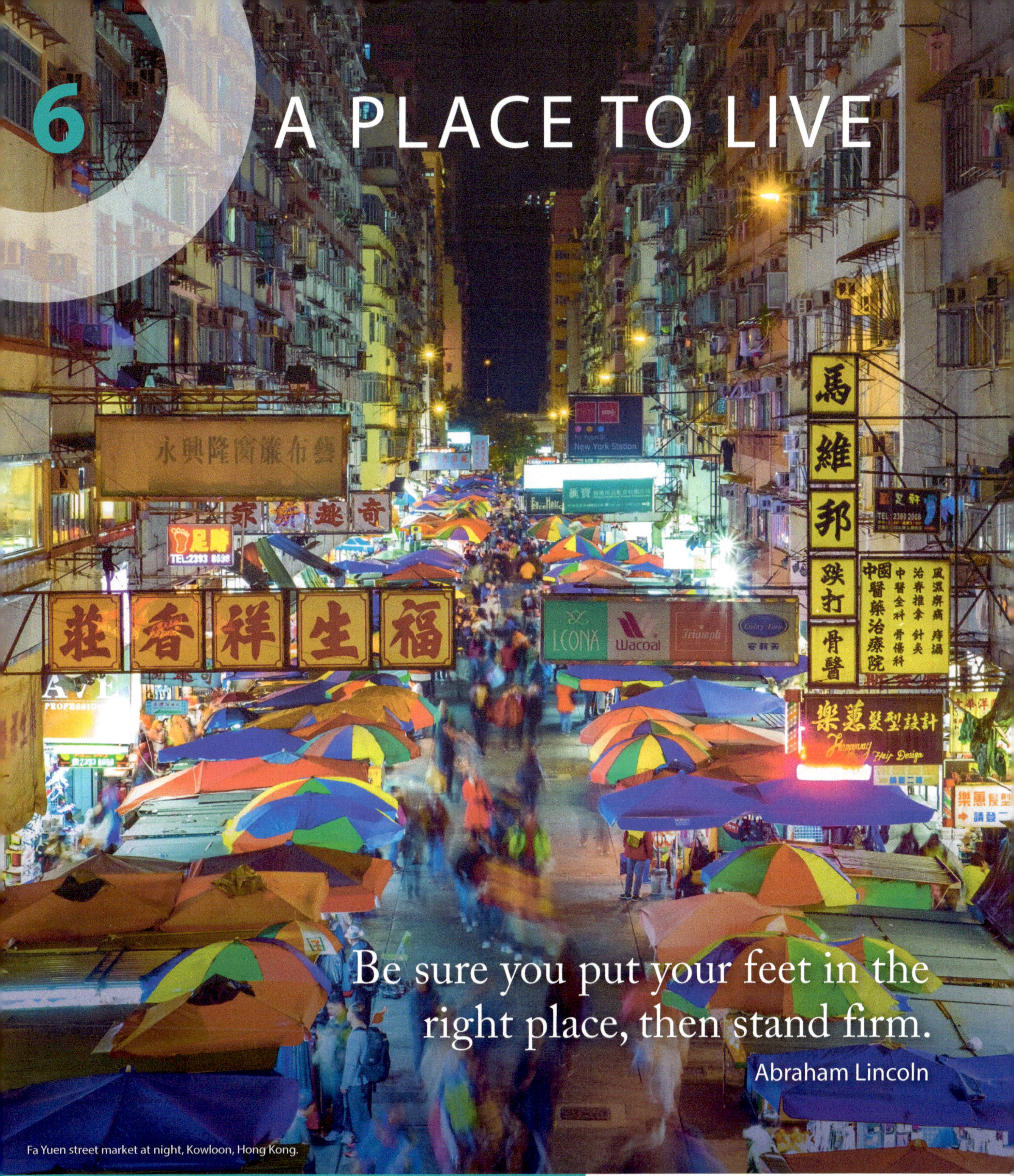

Be sure you put your feet in the right place, then stand firm.

Abraham Lincoln

Fa Yuen street market at night, Kowloon, Hong Kong.

OBJECTIVES

- describe your town or city
- describe your home
- ask for and give directions
- write a review of a café

Work with a partner. Discuss the questions.

1 Where do you live?
2 Look at the picture. Is this a good place to live? Why/Why not?
3 Complete the sentence in your own words:
Life in a big city is … because …

cheap dangerous difficult easy
expensive horrible nice safe

6.1 Around town

Describe your town or city

V places in a town G *there is / there are; some* and *any* P *there is / there are*

VOCABULARY

Places in a town

6.1 **A** Match the places (1–10) with the words in the box. Then listen and check your answers.

art gallery café hotel market museum park restaurant store station theater

1 ________

2 ________

3 ________

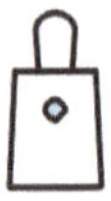
4 ________

5 ________

6 ________

7 ________

8 ________

9 ________

10 ________

6.1 **B** Listen and repeat.

C Complete the sentences with the names of places in a town.

1 I sometimes go to the ________ on the weekend to see a play.
2 We usually buy fresh fruits and vegetables at the ________.
3 Let's visit the ________ to see the paintings.
4 We frequently visit the ________ to learn about history.
5 Let's go out to a ________ for dinner tonight!
6 We frequently stay in a ________ on vacation.
7 I usually take my children to the ________ to play soccer.
8 Let's go to a ________ for some coffee and ice cream!
9 Suzanna frequently goes to the ________ to buy clothes or shoes.
10 How far is it to the ________? My train is at 3 pm.

D SPEAK Work in pairs. Which of these places do you go to in your town?

READING

A PREPARE TO READ Look at the pictures in *What's special about your home town?* Find these things in the pictures.

boat bridge building canal market

B READ FOR GIST Read *What's special about your home town?* Choose the best summary of the main idea.

a Only tourists enjoy Venice.
b Venice is a very difficult place to live.
c Life in Venice is interesting and fun.

C READ FOR GIST Which topics are in the forum post? Check (✓) the answers.

☐ art ☐ food ☐ hotels ☐ jobs
☐ music ☐ schools ☐ transportation

D READ FOR DETAIL Are the sentences true (T) or false (F)?

1 Venice is a modern city. T / F
2 Venice is a good city to see art. T / F
3 There are hundreds of bridges in Venice. T / F
4 There are a lot of cars and buses in the city center. T / F
5 The writer takes a water taxi to work. T / F

E SPEAK Work in groups. Answer the questions.

1 Is Venice a good place to live, in your opinion? Why/Why not?
2 Is Venice similar to or different from your home town or city?

What's special about
YOUR HOME TOWN?

March 17, 6:57 Reply | Like

I live in Venice, in Italy. It's famous all over the world and there are a lot of tourists. But it's an exciting place to live and work, too.

GRAMMAR

there is / there are; some and any

A Read the post again. Underline examples of *there is, there are, some* and *any*.

B **WORK IT OUT** Complete the table using the examples in Exercise A to help you.

there is / there are; some and any		
	Singular	Plural
Positive +	There [1] ______ really good café.	There [2] ______ over 400 bridges.
Negative -	There [3] ______ really large grocery store..	There [4] ______ cars.
Some and *a lot of*	We use *some* and *a lot* of with [5]***singular / plural*** nouns. *Some* means a [6]***small / big*** number. *A lot of* means a [7]***small / big*** number. We usually use them in [8]***positive / negative*** sentences.	
Any	We use *any* in [9]***negative / positive*** sentences and in questions.	

C Go to the **Grammar Hub** on **page XVI**.

D **SPEAK** Work in pairs. Talk about places near where you are. Use *there is* or *there are* and the words in the box.

art gallery | cafés | hotel | museum | restaurants | stores

A: There's an art gallery near the school, but there isn't a museum.

B: There are cafés near the school, but there aren't any restaurants.

Venice is a city with a lot of history – I love it! There are some buildings that are over 500 years old! Venice is great for art. There are museums and art galleries everywhere. There are over 400 bridges in Venice. Why? Because there are a lot of canals! There aren't any cars in this area, but there's a train station outside the city center. There aren't any buses in the center either – people go to work by water taxi! There isn't a really large grocery store, but there's a great market with a lot of fresh fruits and vegetables.

I walk to work every morning and look at the buildings and the canals and the bridges. They're amazing! There's a really good café near my home. They make great coffee and fresh sandwiches and I eat breakfast there every morning when I go to work. I think Venice is a great place to live!

PRONUNCIATION

there is / there are

A Read and listen to the examples. 6.2

1 There's a restaurant.
2 There's a grocery store.
3 There are some stores.
4 There are some hotels.

B Listen and repeat the sentences in Exercise A. 6.2

SPEAKING

A **PLAN** Write the names of places in the chart. Use the words from the Vocabulary section on page 42.

Everyday life	Weekend fun	Food and drink
market		

B **PREPARE** Work in pairs. Are these sentences true or false about your town?

1 There are a lot of parks in my town and there's a museum.
2 There aren't any theaters, but there's an art gallery.
3 There's a large grocery store and there are also a lot of small stores.

C **DISCUSS** Work in groups. Talk about places in your town.

There are a lot of parks in my city. There's a big park near the river and I usually go there with my friends on the weekend.

Describe your town or city

6.2 Choosing a home

Describe your home

V – furniture and rooms; prepositions of place
G – *is there / are there* question forms
S – predicting
P – vowel sounds: /ʌ/ and /e/

VOCABULARY

Furniture and rooms

A Look at the picture. What kind of person do you think lives here?

B Complete the description with the words in the box.

bed	bookshelf	chair	clock	closet
cushion	desk	lamp	wall	window

The [1] ________ and the [2] ________ are blue. The [3] ________ is green. The [4] ________ is yellow. The [5] ________ is red. The [6] ________ is big. The [7] ________ is brown. The [8] ________ is gray. The [9] ________ is orange. The [10] ________ is light yellow.

6.3 **C** Listen and check your answers to Exercise B .

D Go to the Vocabulary Hub on page XX.

E **SPEAK** Work in pairs. What furniture do you have in your room at home or your classroom?

Prepositions of place

A Look at the picture in Vocabulary Exercise A again. Complete the description below using *in*, *on* or *under*.

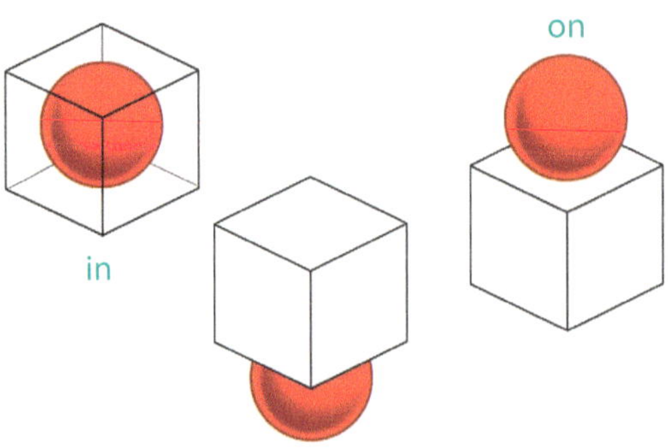

There's a desk and a chair [1] ________ the room. There's a lamp [2] ________ the desk. There are clothes [3] ________ the closet. There are books [4] ________ the bookshelf. There's a small table next to the bed. There's a clock [5] ________ the table. There's a cushion [6] ________ the chair. There's a bag [7] ________ the desk. There's a picture [8] ________ the wall.

6.4 **B** Listen to a description of the room. Find four differences between the picture opposite and the description you hear.

C **SPEAK** Work in pairs. Look at the picture again. Describe the location of one thing. Say the object your partner is describing.

A: It's on the desk.
B: Is it the lamp?

D Student A – Go to the Communication Hub on page XXI. Student B – Go to the Communication Hub on page XXIII.

LISTENING

A **PREPARE TO LISTEN** Read the information about a studio apartment and answer the questions.

1 Where is the studio?
2 What is near the studio?
3 How can you get more information?

> **NYC RENTALS**
> **Studio** for rent in central Manhattan.
> Close to a bus stop and a grocery store.
> Must see! Call for an appointment.
> **646-755-8318**

> **Predicting**
> Before you listen, try to think about which topics will be in the conversation. Predicting helps to make the information easier to understand.

B **PREDICT** Look at the form in Exercise D. Check (✓) the topics that you think you will hear in the conversation.

☐ location ☐ neighbors ☐ number of rooms
☐ pets ☐ money ☐ stores ☐ size

6.5 **C** **LISTEN FOR GIST** Listen to the conversation and check your answers to Exercise B. Does the man decide to rent the apartment?

6.5 **D** **LISTEN FOR DETAIL** Listen to the conversation again. Complete the form with the correct information.

> **STUDIO FOR RENT**
> Address: ________ East 23rd Street
> Time to bus stop: ________ minutes
> Furniture:
> ☐ desk ☐ chair ☐ bookshelf
> ☐ lamp ☐ closet ☐ couch
> ☐ armchair ☐ bed
> Window with view of ________
> Bathroom: **yes/no** Kitchen: **yes/no**
> Price per month: ________

6.5 **E** **LISTEN FOR DETAIL** Listen again. Why doesn't the man like the room?

GRAMMAR

is there / are there question forms

A Complete the sentences with the correct form of *be* and the words in the box.

a bathroom (✓) buses (✓) chairs (✗) a kitchen (✗)

1. Is there ___ ________________?
   Yes, there ________________.
2. Are there any ________________?
   Yes, there ________________.
3. Is there ___ ________________?
   No, there ________________.
4. Are there any ________________?
   No, there ________________.

B **WORK IT OUT** Choose the correct options to complete the rules. Use the examples in Exercise A to help you.

is there / are there question forms

To make *yes/no* questions, we put *is* or *are* [1]***before / after*** *there*.

We use *any* in questions with [2]***singular / plural*** nouns.

We [3]***use / don't use*** the contracted form of *there is* (*there's*) in short answers.

C Go to the **Grammar Hub** on **page XVI**.

D **SPEAK** Work in pairs. Ask your partner about their room at home. Use the words in the box.

books bookshelf clock cushions desk lamp pictures window

A: Are there any books in your room?
B: Yes, there are a lot of books. They're on a bookshelf.

PRONUNCIATION

Vowel sounds: /ʌ/ and /e/

6.6 **A** Listen to the sounds /ʌ/ and /e/.

/ʌ/ rug /e/ bed

6.7 **B** Listen and circle the words with the same vowel sound as the word in bold.

1. **/ʌ/ rug**

   son run song some love blog

2. **/e/ bed**

   get clean red sad bread head

6.8 **C** Listen and circle the word you hear.

1. There's a *bag / bug* on the floor.
2. This is a *bad room / bedroom*.
3. Is there a *pen / pan* in the kitchen?
4. Be careful with that *cut / cat*!

SPEAKING HUB

A **PREPARE** You want to rent a room from your partner. Student A – Stay on this page. Student B – Go to the **Communication Hub** on **page XXIV**. Read the description of what you need. Write five questions to ask your partner.

a desk	*Is there a desk?*
chairs	________________
a lamp	________________
a TV	________________
near a bus stop or train station	________________
near a grocery store	________________

B **DISCUSS** Ask your partner questions about their room. Find out if it is the right place for you.

A: Can I ask about the room for rent?
B: Yes, of course. How can I help you?
A: Is it near a bus stop?
B: No, it isn't. But there's a train station ten minutes away.

C **REPEAT** Answer your partner's questions. Use the information in the advertisement.

Your room:

- Comfortable room in quiet area.
- Near museums, theaters and restaurants.
- Large window with view of the street.
- Bed, table, chair and lamp included.
- Free internet included.

$200 per week

D **REPORT** Tell the class about the room.

I like / don't like my partner's room because …

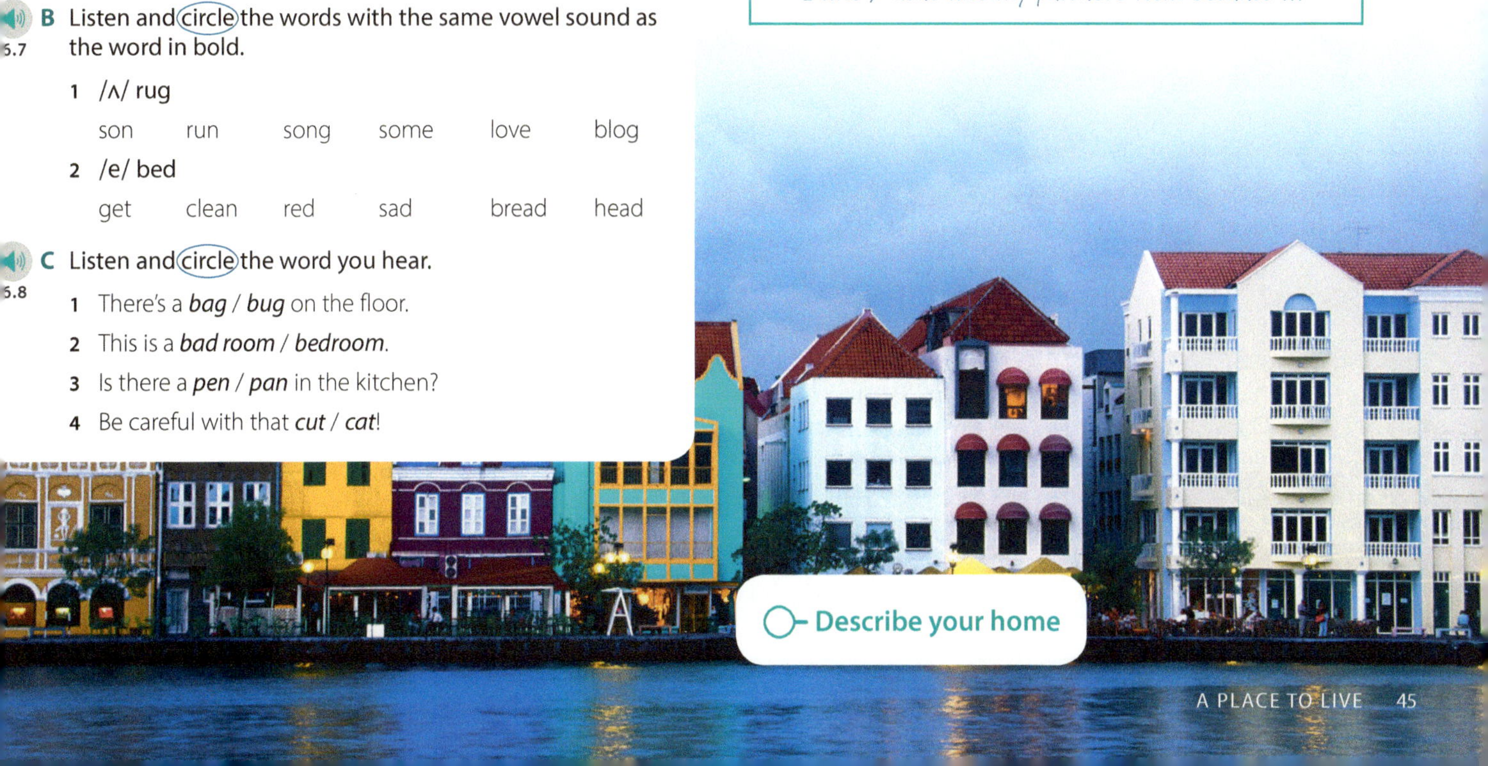

Describe your home

Café Hub

6.3 Left or right?

F – ask for and give directions

COMPREHENSION

A Watch the video. Are the sentences true (T) or false (F)? Correct the false sentences.

1 Gaby wants to take photos in the park. *T / F*
2 Sam gives directions to the park. *T / F*
3 Newton Green park is near Sam's Café. *T / F*
4 The three men in the café are friends. *T / F*
5 Gaby asks her phone for directions. *T / F*

B Watch the video and match the locations of the park (a, b or c) with the three men (1, 2 and 3).

Man 1 ___

Man 2 ___

Man 3 ___

USEFUL PHRASES

A Who says it? Sam, Man 1, Man 2 or Man 3?

1 Yes, it's very near. ________
2 OK everybody, let's just relax. ________
3 You're both wrong. ________
4 Yes, calm down! ________
5 I'm not sure. ________

B Complete the conversation with useful phrases from Exercise A.

Gaby: Is there a park near here?
Sam: A park … [1] ________________
Man 1: Actually, there is a park near here. Newton Green.
Gaby: Newton Green.
Man 1: [2] ________________ Go out of the café, turn left, then cross the road, then turn right.
Man 2: No, no, no. Go out of the café, turn left and cross the road. But then, turn left, not right.
Man 1: No, it's right.
Man 2: No, it's left.
Man 1: Right.
Man 2: Left.
Sam: [3] ________________
Man 3: [4] ________________
[5] ________________

C 00:24–01:21 Watch part of the video again and check your answers.

GABY

SAM

LUCY

FUNCTIONAL LANGUAGE

Asking for and giving directions

A Complete the phrases with the words in the box.

Cross Go left near on out there Turn

Asking for directions

Is [1] __________ a park [2] __________ here?

Giving directions

Go [3] __________ of the café.	
Turn [4] __________.	
[5] __________ right.	
[6] __________ the street.	
[7] __________ straight ahead.	
The park is [8] __________ your left.	

B Look at the map of the town in the Speaking section. Complete the correct directions to go from Sam's Café to Newton Green.

Go [1] __________ of the café and turn [2] __________. Then turn [3] __________ and go [4] __________. Then turn [5] __________ and then turn [6] __________. The park is on your [7] __________.

PRONUNCIATION

6.9 **A** Listen to the conversation and notice how the underlined words are stressed.

James: Is there a restaurant near here?

Sarah: Yes. Go out of the café and turn right. Then turn right and go straight ahead. Then turn right again and then turn left. The restaurant is on your left.

James: So, I go out of the café and turn right.

Sarah: Yes. Then turn right and go straight ahead.

James: Then turn right again and then left and the restaurant is on my left. Perfect.

6.9 **B** Work in pairs. Listen again and repeat the conversation. Copy the stress.

C SPEAK Work in pairs. Practice the conversation in Exercise A.

SPEAKING

A PREPARE Work in pairs. Take turns asking for and giving directions from Sam's Café. Use the map below.

A: Is there a movie theater near here?

B: Yes. Go out of Sam's Café and turn left. Then turn left and then left again. The movie theater is on your left.

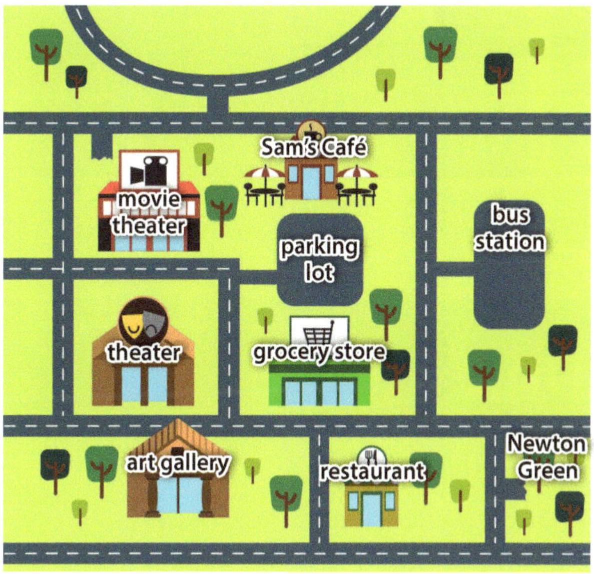

B PRACTICE Work in groups of three. Write and practice a conversation. Use the map above or use a local map. Include three or more useful phrases.

Student A

- Ask for directions to a place on the map.

Student B

- Give wrong directions.

Student C

- Disagree and give the correct directions.

C PRESENT Perform your conversation for the class. Which conversation is the best?

Ask for and give directions

6 Writing

Write a review of a café

W– using *because*

A Work in pairs. Describe the picture. Use the words in the box to help you.

chair floor lamp table wall window

B Read the text. Why did the writer write it?

a to ask people to visit the café
b to say what he thinks about the café
c to tell the story of his visit to the café

Amazing hot chocolate! ★★★★☆

I love this café because it's modern and clean. There are really cool chairs and tables. The hot chocolate is excellent, but it's a little expensive! It's usually very busy and I sometimes wait 20 minutes or more for my hot chocolate. There's free internet so it's the perfect place to read your emails and text messages.

♡ 7 ⟲ 2

C Read the text again. What are the positive and negative things about the café?

Positive	Negative

Using *because*

We use *because* to give reasons and answer the question *why?*

I love this café ***because*** it's modern and clean.

D SPEAK Work in pairs. What is your opinion of this café?

WRITING

A PREPARE Think of a café that you like or don't like. Complete the table with your reasons.

Like	Dislike

B WRITE Write a short review of your café. Use the review in Exercise B as a model.

C PRESENT Read your review to your partner. Listen to your partner. When they finish ask questions for more information.

Write a review of a café

Unit 6 Review

GRAMMAR

A Choose the correct options to complete the sentences.

1 *There's / There are* three theaters in my town.
2 *Are there / There are* any art galleries?
3 There aren't any *stores / park*.
4 *There's / Is there* a new café near my home.
5 **A:** Is there a market?
B: Yes, *there is / there's*.

B Complete the conversation with the correct form of *there is* or *there are*.

Aya: Please tell me about your new apartment. [1] ____________ a living room?
Kay: Yes, [2] ____________ a living room. [3] ____________ also two bedrooms.
Aya: [4] ____________ any stores nearby?
Kay: No, [5] ____________. But [6] ____________ a large grocery store near the station.

VOCABULARY

A Complete the words to describe places in a town.

1 I always buy fresh food at the m _ _ _ _ _.
2 My friends sometimes play soccer in the p _ _ _.
3 They usually stay in a h _ _ _ _ when they go on vacation.
4 I go to the s _ _ _ _ _ _ every morning at 8 am to get the train.
5 We sometimes eat dinner at a r _ _ _ _ _ _ _ _ near our house.

B Complete the sentences with prepositions of place and words for furniture.

There are two chairs and a desk in this room. There's a cushion [1] ____________ one chair. There's a bag [2] ____________ the other chair. There's a [3] ____________ and a [4] ____________ on the desk. There are books on the [5] ____________. There's a mirror [6] ____________ the wall. There are some clothes in the [7] ____________. There's a small [8] ____________ on the floor.

Endmatter Contents

Grammar Hub

Vocabulary Hub

Communication Hub

Grammar Hub

1.1

Simple present *be*: *I, you*

	Positive	Negative
I	**I am** from Germany.	**I am not** from Germany.
	I'm from Germany.	**I'm not** from Germany.
you	**You are** from Canada.	**You are not** from Canada.
	You're from Canada.	**You aren't** from Canada.
		You're not from Canada.

	Yes/No questions	Short answers
you	**Are you** from Argentina?	**Yes, I am.**
		No, I'm not.

- For the verb *be*, we use *am* with *I* and *are* with *you*.

  I am happy.
  You are happy.

- We can use the long form (*I am / You are*) or the contraction (*I'm/You're*). We typically use the contraction when we speak.

  I am from London. OR I'm from London.
  You are from France. OR You're from France.

Be careful!

- Remember: I am = I'm, You are = You're.

  I'm from Peru. NOT ~~I'm am from Peru.~~
  You're from Brazil. NOT ~~You're are from Brazil.~~

1.2

Simple present *be*: *he, she, it*

	Positive	Negative
he/she/it	**He/She is** a teacher.	**He/She is not** a teacher.
	He's/She's a teacher.	**He/She isn't** a teacher.
		He's/She's not a teacher.
	It is small.	**It is not** small.
	It's small.	**It isn't** small.
		It's not small.

	Yes/No questions	Short answers
he/she/it	**Is he** friendly?	**Yes, he is. / No, he isn't.**
	Is she the manager?	**Yes, she is. / No, she isn't.**
	Is it fun?	**Yes, it is. / No, it isn't.**

- For the verb *be*, we use *is* with *he*, *she* and *it*.

  He is nice.
  She is nice.
  It is nice.

- We can use the long form (*He is / She is / It is*) or the contraction (*He's / She's / It's*). We typically use the contraction when we speak.

  He is busy. OR He's busy.
  She is happy at her job. OR She's happy at her job.
  It is a big company. OR It's a big company.

Be careful!

- For negative short answers, we usually use the contraction.

  No, she isn't. NOT ~~No, she is not.~~

1.1

Simple present *be*: *I, you*

A Choose the correct options.

1 I (*am*) / *are* from Madrid.
2 *You're* / *You're are* from Sweden.
3 *I not* / *I'm not* from Berlin.
4 You *not* / *aren't* from Hungary.
5 *You are* / *Are you* from New York?
6 I *are* / *am* from Germany.
7 You *are* / *am* from the UK.
8 *Am* / *Are* you from Indonesia?

B Write the negatives. Use contractions.

1 I'm from Italy.
I'm not from Italy.
2 You're from Brazil.
______
3 I'm from China.
______
4 You're from Egypt.
______
5 I'm from Japan.
______
6 You're from Turkey.
______
7 I'm from Mexico.
______
8 You're from Australia.
______

C Complete the conversations with the words in the box.

am ~~are~~ I I'm no not yes you

1 **A:** *Are* you from Italy?
B: Yes, I am.
2 **A:** Hello. Are you from Brazil?
B: Yes, I ______.
3 **A:** Are ______ from Australia?
B: Yes, I am.
4 **A:** Are you from Morocco?
B: ______, I am.
5 **A:** Are you from Canada?
B: ______, I'm not.
6 **A:** Good morning. Are you from Argentina?
B: Yes, ______ am.
7 **A:** Hello Lisa. Are you from China?
B: No, I'm ______.
8 **A:** Are you from Mexico?
B: No, ______ not.

➤ Go back to page 3.

1.2

Simple present *be*: *he, she, it*

A Choose the correct options.

1 He ___ an architect.
a be (b) is
2 My friend is ___ a doctor.
a not b isn't
3 Maria is a manager. ___ very nice.
a It's b She's
4 I like my job. ___ fun.
a It's b She's
5 Paul isn't a teacher. ___ a student.
a He's b It's
6 Her name ___ Karen and she's from Canada.
a is b are

B Complete the email with the words in the box.

he's is (x4) ~~isn't~~ it's she's

Hi Tina!

I'm at work but I'm not very busy. My manager [1] *isn't* here today because she [2] ______ in New York City. Her name [3] ______ Sandra and [4] ______ very nice. The job [5] ______ fun and I'm very happy here. Henri [6] ______ my colleague. [7] ______ very friendly. We're on the design team. [8] ______ a small team with four people.

See you soon!

Love,

Annette

C Write the correct short answers.

1 **A:** Is Marco a manager?
B: *No, he isn't.* (-)
2 **A:** Is your job difficult?
B: ______ (-)
3 **A:** Is Peter a student?
B: ______ (+)
4 **A:** Is Tina a teacher?
B: ______ (-)
5 **A:** Is your job fun?
B: ______ (+)

➤ Go back to page 5.

Grammar Hub

2.1

Simple present *be*: *we, you, they*

	Positive	Negative
we	**We are** from New York. **We're** from New York.	**We are not** from Canada. **We aren't** from Canada. **We're not** from Canada.
you	**You are** from Italy. **You're** from Italy.	**You are not** Spanish. **You aren't** Spanish. **You're not** Spanish.
they	**They are** Norwegian. **They're** Norwegian.	**They are not** from Sweden. **They aren't** from Sweden. **They're not** from Sweden.

	Yes/No questions	Short answers
we	**Are we** a great band?	**Yes, you are. / No, you aren't. / No, you're not.**
you	**Are you** musicians?	**Yes, we are. / No, we aren't. / No, we're not.**
they	**Are they** fans of world music?	**Yes, they are. / No, they aren't. / No, they're not.**

- For the verb *be*, we use *are* after the pronouns *we*, *you* and *they*.
  We are from Senegal. We're from Senegal.
  They aren't in a band.
- In *yes/no* questions, the verb *be* is first.
  Are they good at music?
  Are we at the concert?
- The answer to a *yes/no* question is *yes* or *no*, followed by a pronoun and the verb *be*.
  Are you from America? Yes, we are. / No, we aren't. / No, we're not.
  Are they singers? Yes, they are. / No, they aren't. / No, they're not.
- In *yes/no* questions with *no* answers, we can write the contraction in two ways.
  Are they from Boston? No, they aren't. OR No, they're not.

Be careful!

- In *yes/no* questions with *yes* answers, we cannot write the contraction.
  Are you fans of the band? Yes, we are.
  NOT ~~Yes, we're.~~

Possessive adjectives

Subject pronoun	Possessive adjective
I am a fan of American music.	**My** playlist is very cool.
You are from Japan.	**Your** country is in Asia.
He is Malian.	**His** country is in Africa.
We are from France.	**Our** country is in Europe.
They are singers.	**Their** songs are really good.

- For possessive adjectives, we change the subject pronoun to the correct possessive adjective.
  *I'm in a band. **My** band's name is Full Energy.*
  *We are from Poland. **Our** country is quite big.*

2.2

Wh-* questions with *be

Question word	*be*	Rest of question	Answer
What	**is**	your name?	**My name is** Lee.
Where	**are**	you from?	**I am** from China.
Who	**is**	your teacher?	**Our teacher is** Ms. Daniels.
When	**is**	your class?	**It's at** 10 am.
How old	**are**	your friends?	**They are** 14 years old.

- In *wh-* questions, the question word is first.
  What are their jobs?
  Where am I right now?
- In *wh-* questions, the verb is second.
  Who is your classmate?
  Where are Jason and Alex?

Be careful!

- In *wh-* questions, the verb matches the noun after it. The noun is the subject of the *wh-* question.
  Where is their house? NOT ~~Where are their house?~~
  What are your names? NOT ~~What is your names?~~

2.1

Simple present *be*: *we, you, they*; possessive adjectives

A Choose the correct options.

1 Niko and John are Greek. ***They*** / ***We*** are from Greece.
2 My best friend and I are Icelandic. ***You*** / ***We*** are from Iceland.
3 ***You are*** / ***Are you*** from Portugal?
4 Are you fans of his music? Yes, ***I*** / ***we*** are.
5 Are your friends from Chile? Yes, ***we*** / ***they*** are.
6 Are they free tonight? ***No, they're not.*** / ***Yes, they're.***
7 I'm a fan of music. ***My*** / ***Your*** playlist is full of songs.
8 We're from Italy. ***Our*** / ***Their*** country is in southern Europe.

B Put the words in the correct order to make sentences and questions.

1 from / your friends / are / Jamaica
Are your friends from Jamaica ?
2 fans / we / of / her / music / aren't
_______________.
3 great / their / are / songs
_______________?
4 from / are / they / Reykjavik
_______________?
5 are / you / favorite / my / singer
_______________!
6 big fans / new album / they're / their / of
_______________.
7 classmates / are / Italian / your
_______________?
8 from / they're / Turkey / not
_______________.

C Choose the correct options to complete the conversation.

Samantha: Hi, I'm Samantha. [1] ___ in my music class?
Henry: Hi, Samantha. I'm Henry. Yes, [2] ___ in the class together.
Samantha: Great! [3] ___ a big fan of music like me?
Henry: Oh, yes. [4] ___ playlist is full of great songs.
Samantha: That's nice. [5] ___ teacher is really nice, too.
Henry: Yes, I'm excited about [6] ___ lessons.
Samantha: Well, see you in class!
Henry: Bye!

1 (a) Are you b You are
2 a we're b are we
3 a You're b Are you
4 a Your b My
5 a Our b His
6 a your b my

➤ Go back to page 11.

2.2

Wh-* questions with *be

A Choose the correct options.

1 What ___ your name?
(a) is b are
2 Who ___ your best friends?
a is b are
3 Where ___ your teacher from?
a is b are
4 How old ___ your parents?
a is b are
5 ___ your favorite artist?
a What's b Who's
6 ___ your favorite song?
a Where's b What's

B Write the correct form of the verb *be* to complete the questions.

1 Where ____are____ Tom and Joseph?
2 What ________ her nationality?
3 Who ________ your favorite musicians?
4 How old ________ Shannon and Michael?
5 What ________ his favorite apps?
6 Who ________ Ariana Grande?
7 How old ________ this movie?
8 When ________ your class?

C Match the questions (1–8) and the answers (a–h).

1 Where are Zara and Aliyah from? g
2 Who's your Japanese teacher? ___
3 What's your favorite language? ___
4 How old is your new classmate? ___
5 Where's Karen from? ___
6 How old are your sisters? ___
7 Who are your neighbors? ___
8 When's your class? ___

a It's on Wednesday.
b He's 14.
c They're Mr. and Mrs. Neilson.
d She's from Sweden.
e It's Chinese.
f Mr. Watanabe.
g They're from Egypt.
h They're 24 and 28.

➤ Go back to page 13.

Grammar Hub

3.1

a/an* and plural nouns; *this, that, these, those

a/an	Plural nouns
a hat	three hat**s**
a phone	phone**s**
a box	two box**es**
a baby	three bab**ies**
an umbrella	two umbrella**s**

- We use *a* or *an* to talk about one object.
- We use *an* when the noun starts with a vowel sound (*a, e, i, o, u*). We use *a* when the noun doesn't start with a vowel sound.
- We don't use *a* or *an* with plural nouns (= more than one object).
- We add -*s* to the end of most nouns to make them plural.
- We add -*es* to the end of nouns ending in -*ch* (e.g. *watch – watches*), -*s* or -*ss* (e.g. *class – classes*), -*sh* (e.g. *brush – brushes*), -*x* (e.g. *box – boxes*), and -*o* (e.g. *potato – potatoes*) to make them plural.
- For nouns ending in -*y*, we change the -*y* to -*i*- and add -*es* (e.g. *baby* – babies).

this, that, these, those

- We use *this* and *that* to talk about one object.

  Is this your bag?
- We use *these* and *those* to talk about more than one object.

  Those actors are Italian.
- We use *this* and *these* to talk about things that are near.

  These are my shoes.
- We use *that* and *those* to talk about things that are not near.

  That's Khaled's house over there.

3.2

have/has

	Positive	Negative
I/you/we/they	**I have** a phone. **You have** a phone. **We have** a phone. **They have** a phone.	**I don't have** a son. **You don't have** a son. **We don't have** a son. **They don't have** a son.
he/she	**He has** a phone. **She has** a phone.	**He doesn't have** an umbrella.

	Question	Short answers
I/you/we/they	**Do I/you/we/they have** children?	**Yes, I/you/we/they do.** **No, I/you/we/they don't.**
he/she	**Does he/she have** a red bag?	**Yes, he/she does.** **No, he/she doesn't.**

- We use *have/has* to talk about family members and things that we own.

3.1

a/an and plural nouns

A Choose *a* or *an* or no article (–) to complete the sentences and questions.

1 My grandmother has ***a*** / ***an*** / (–) glasses.
2 ***A*** / ***An*** / – headphones are useful.
3 Aisha doesn't have ***a*** / ***an*** / – coat.
4 Is there ***a*** / ***an*** / – address on the letter?
5 This is ***a*** / ***an*** / – map of Turkey.
6 Take ***a*** / ***an*** / – umbrella with you!

B Complete the sentences and questions with the plural form of the words in parentheses.

1 Put three ___*tomatoes*___ (*tomato*) in the salad.
2 Our ______________ (*family*) live on the same street.
3 When are your piano ______________ (*lesson*)?
4 Which ______________ (*country*) are on the map?
5 My team isn't playing well – we have five ______________ (*loss*)!

this, that, these, those

C Complete the sentences and questions with *is* or *are*.

1 This phone ___*is*___ great!
2 ______________ that a map of Greece?
3 These ______________ my new shoes.
4 These exercises ______________ easy!
5 What ______________ that thing over there?
6 ______________ these Olivia's headphones?

D Read the sentences and check (✓) the correct pictures.

1 This is my new hat.

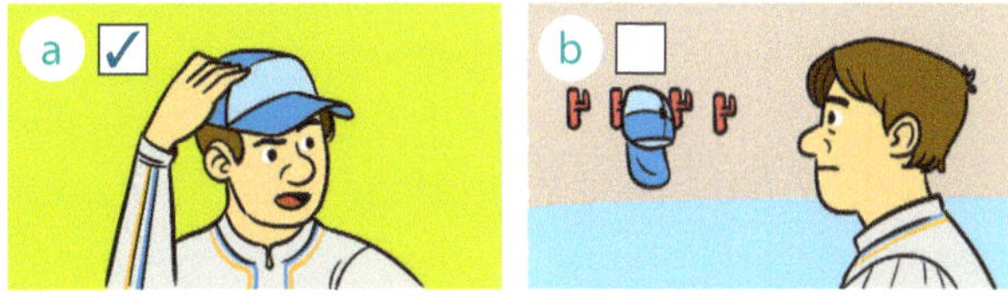

2 That is my book.

3 Those headphones are cool!

4 Are these your keys?

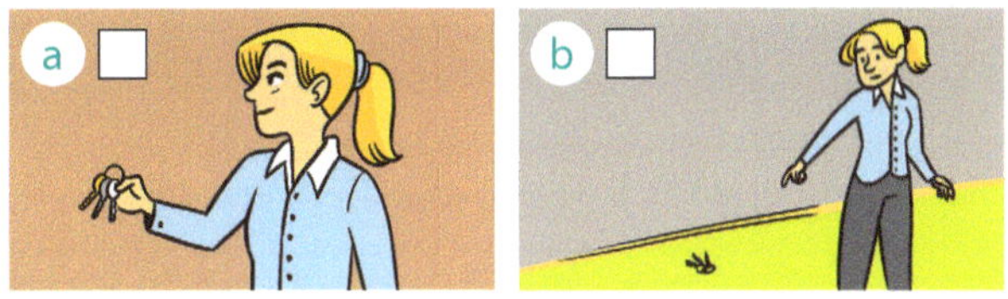

➤ Go back to page 19.

3.2

have/has

A Complete the sentences with the correct form of *have*.

1 Afua ___*doesn't have*___ a coat and she's cold! (-)
2 My friends and I ______________ English classes on Sundays. (-)
3 My mother ______________ a new phone. (+)
4 I ______________ a brother. (+)
5 Akim ______________ a blue school bag. (+)
6 My dad ______________ glasses. (-)
7 She ______________ a brother and a sister. (+)
8 We ______________ a new car. (+)
9 They ______________ grandchildren. (-)
10 Sarah ______________ a coat. (-)

B Put the words in order to make questions. Then write short answers.

1 my phone / have / Do / you
A: *Do you have my phone*______________?
B: No, ___*I don't*___.

2 have / Carlo / a brother / Does
A: ______________?
B: No, ______________.

3 have / they / a red car / Do
A: ______________?
B: Yes, ______________.

4 two grandchildren / Mary and John / have / Do
A: ______________?
B: Yes, ______________.

5 the waiter / have / our food / Does
A: ______________?
B: Yes, ______________.

➤ Go back to page 21.

Grammar Hub

4.1

Simple present: *I, you, we, they*

	Positive	Negative
I	**I work** in an office.	**I do not work** in an office. **I don't work** in an office.
you	**You start** work at eight o'clock.	**You do not start** work at eight o'clock. **You don't start** work at eight o'clock.
we	**We watch** TV in the evening.	**We do not watch** TV in the evening. **We don't watch** TV in the evening.
they	**They play** soccer.	**They do not play** soccer. **They don't play** soccer.

- We use the simple present for things that are always true or actions that always happen.

  They live in a lighthouse.
  We play soccer on Saturdays.
- For *I/you/we/they*, the verb form is the same.

  I play.
  We play.
- We form the negative with the long form (*do not*) or the contraction (*don't*) before the verb. We usually use the contraction when we speak.

  I do not start work at nine o'clock. OR I don't start work at nine o'clock.

Be careful!

- Remember that *don't* is the negative of *do not*.

  I don't work here. NOT ~~I don't not work here.~~

4.2

Simple present questions: *I, you, we, they*

	Yes/No question	Positive short answer	Negative short answer
I	**Do I** live in a house?	**Yes, you do.**	**No, you don't.**
you	**Do you go** to the river?	**Yes, I/we do.**	**No, I/we don't.**
we	**Do we live** in houses?	**Yes, you do.**	**No, you don't.**
they	**Do they go** to the countryside?	**Yes, they do.**	**No, they don't.**

	Wh- questions
I/you/we/they	**What time do I start** work? **How do you relax**? **Where do we live**? **When do they go** to work?

- For *yes/no* questions, we put *do* at the beginning. We don't change the verb.

  Do you work here?
- For other questions we can use question words, e.g. *where, when, what time, who, how*, etc. We put *do* after the question word.

  Where do you live?
  When do we start work?

Be careful!

- For negative answers to *yes/no* questions, we normally use the contraction.

  No, I don't. NOT ~~No, I do not.~~

4.1

Simple present: *I, you, we, they*

A Choose the correct options.

1 I (*don't*) / *not* watch TV in the mornings.
2 They *do go* / *go* to bed at 11 pm.
3 After work, we go home and *to relax* / *relax*.
4 I *don't* / *not* get up early on Sundays.
5 I *am live* / *live* with two friends.
6 We *start* / *do start* work at seven in the morning.
7 You *go* / *to go* out on Saturdays.
8 They *play don't* / *don't play* games on their computers at work.

B Complete the text with the verbs in the box.

don't talk finish get up go live relax start ~~work~~

I [1] ___work___ in an office. My friends Anna and Frieda work there too. They're very nice. We [2] ________ work at 8 am, so I [3] ________ at 7 am. When we [4] ________ work – at about five o'clock, we [5] ________ out. Our other friends [6] ________ in the town, so we meet them after work. We [7] ________ and we [8] ________ about work!

C Reorder the words to make sentences.

1 don't / at six o'clock / I / get up ___I don't get up at six o'clock___.
2 TV / in the evenings / watch / I ________.
3 at seven o'clock / work / don't / you / start ________.
4 live / we / in the same house ________.
5 games / on my computer / play / I ________.
6 on Monday evenings / don't / we / go out ________.
7 they / here / don't / live ________.
8 I / at home / relax ________.

➤ Go back to page 27.

4.2

Simple present questions: *I, you, we, they*

A Match the questions (1–6) and the answers (a–f).

1 Do you live in Texas? ___c___
2 When do we start work? ___
3 Where do they live? ___
4 Do they work in August? ___
5 How do you relax? ___
6 Who do you work with? ___

a In Madrid.
b I watch TV.
c Yes, I do.
d No, they don't.
e Erica.
f At six o'clock.

B Complete the sentences with the words in the box.

do (x2) don't how when where

1 **A:** Do you both live in Warsaw?
B: Yes, we ___do___.
2 **A:** ________ do you live?
B: In Switzerland.
3 **A:** Do those people work with you?
B: No, they ________.
4 **A:** ________ do you get to work?
B: By car.
5 **A:** ________ do you watch TV?
B: In the evening.
6 **A:** Do you go to bed late?
B: Yes, I ________. I go to bed at about one o'clock in the morning.

C Use the prompts to write questions.

1 you / live / in a tent ___Do you live in a tent___?
2 where / you / work ________?
3 you / play / games ________?
4 when / you / talk / to your family ________?
5 what time / you / start work ________?
6 your friends / live here ________?
7 how / we / play this game ________?
8 you / go / to the countryside ________?

➤ Go back to page 29.

Grammar Hub

5.1

Simple present: *he, she, it*

	Positive	Negative
he/she/it	**He cooks** dinner every day. **She washes** the dishes after dinner.	**He doesn't go running** in the morning. **She doesn't do** the laundry every day.

	Yes/No question	Short answer
he/she/it	**Does Henry take** a bath in the evening? **Does it clean** the floor?	**Yes, he does. / No, he doesn't.** **Yes, it does. / No, it doesn't.**

- In positive sentences with *he*, *she* or *it*, we use the main verb plus *-s* or *-es*.

  He cooks dinner for his family.
  She does housework in the afternoon.
- In negative sentences with *he*, *she* or *it*, we use *doesn't* plus the main verb without *-s*.

  Brad doesn't clean the bathroom.
  She doesn't watch TV all the time.
- In *yes/no* questions with *he*, *she* or *it*, we use *does* followed by the subject and the main verb without *-s*.

  Does your mom do your laundry for you?
- In *wh-* questions with *he*, *she* or *it*, we use a subject and *does* plus the main verb without *-s*.

  When does Martin make his bed?
- We use *does* in short answers to *yes/no* questions. We do not repeat the main verb.

  Does Tom clean the kitchen? Yes, he does. NOT ~~*Yes, he does clean.*~~

Be careful!

- Some verbs take *-es* for the ending in *he/she/it* simple present. Some examples are *do* and *go* and verbs that end in *-sh* or *-ch*.

  He does the laundry at night. NOT ~~*He dos the laundry at night.*~~
  She washes dishes with her sister. NOT ~~*She washs dishes with her sister.*~~

5.2

Adverbs of frequency

Adverb (100% → 0%)	Examples with *be*	Examples with other verbs
always	I'm **always** hungry!	I **always** drink coffee with breakfast.
usually	He's **usually** thirsty after running.	He **usually** eats dinner at 7 pm.
frequently	They're **frequently** late for dinner.	They **frequently** eat lunch in their office.
sometimes	You're **sometimes** tired and hungry.	You **sometimes** have coffee after lunch.
seldom	We are **seldom** free for coffee.	You **seldom** have dessert.
never	I'm **never** late for dinner.	I **never** drink orange juice.

- We put adverbs of frequency after the verb *be*.

  He's usually very hungry before lunch.
  They're sometimes busy on weekends.
- We put adverbs of frequency before other verbs.

  I usually have a large salad for supper.
  She frequently drinks water at lunchtime.
- We can also put the adverbs *usually* and *sometimes* at the beginning of the sentence.

  Usually, I have fruit for my breakfast.
  Sometimes, I have coffee.

Be careful!

- We don't put the adverbs *always*, *seldom* or *never* at the beginning of a sentence.

  She always has rice. NOT ~~*Always, she has rice.*~~

Be careful!

- We do not use *never* with *don't* or *doesn't*.

  I never eat late at night. NOT ~~*I don't never eat late at night.*~~

5.1

Simple present: *he, she, it*

A Choose the correct options.

1 He ___ for a walk every weekend.
 a go (b) goes
2 She ___ meals for her children.
 a cook b cooks
3 George doesn't ___ in the backyard at night.
 a sit b sits
4 What gym does Monica ___ to?
 a goes b go
5 Does Taylor ___ chess every day?
 a plays b play
6 Does he go running late at night? Yes, he ___.
 a does b runs
7 Kelly ___ TV on Saturday mornings.
 a watchs b watches
8 What time does Jenny ___ a bath?
 a take b takes

B Check (✓) the correct sentences and put an (✗) for the incorrect sentences.

1 David sits in the backyard in the evening. ✓
2 Mike go running every Sunday. ___
3 Jill cooks meals for her family. ___
4 Paula doesn't plays chess every day. ___
5 Does Josh goes to the gym? ___
6 **A:** Does Henry go shopping?
 B: Yes, he does. ___
7 **A:** Does Amy take a bath every day?
 B: No, she doesn't do! ___
8 Where Erika goes for a walk? ___

C Complete the sentences with the correct form of the words in parentheses.

1 Michelle ___sits___ (*sit*) in the backyard in the summer.
2 My dad ________ (*take*) a bath every night.
3 She ________ (*go*) for a walk every weekend.
4 When ________ (*he / do*) the laundry?
5 **A:** Does your grandmother go running?
 B: No, she ________ (*do not*).
6 Lily ________ (*not go*) to the gym.
7 **A:** Does your brother play chess?
 B: Yes, he ________ (*do*).

➤ Go back to page 35.

5.2

Adverbs of frequency

A Choose the correct adverbs of frequency.

1 I ___ have coffee in the morning, but not every day.
 a always (b) frequently
2 She ___ has salad for lunch. She has it three or four times a week.
 a never b frequently
3 He ___ eats eggs for breakfast. He doesn't like them!
 a sometimes b never
4 They ___ have dinner at home, five or six days a week.
 a never b usually
5 She's ___ early for class, two or three times a month.
 a sometimes b always
6 We ___ cook chicken and rice. My wife and I don't like it.
 a never b usually
7 John is ___ busy on Fridays. He has a lot of work on that day.
 a always b never
8 You ___ eat snacks, almost every day of the week!
 a sometimes b frequently

B Choose the correct options to complete the sentences.

1 Mike ***usually has*** / ***has usually*** juice with his cereal.
2 She ***cooks frequently*** / ***frequently cooks*** dinner for the family.
3 They ***frequently are*** / ***are frequently*** late for class.
4 We ***drink never*** / ***never drink*** milk at breakfast.
5 I ***am sometimes*** / ***sometimes am*** hungry for breakfast.
6 He ***seldom eats*** / ***eats seldom*** vegetables.
7 You ***always aren't*** / ***aren't always*** busy for lunch.
8 Helena doesn't ***never*** / ***usually*** eat bananas.

C Put the words in the correct order to make sentences.

1 drink / usually / for / I / breakfast / tea
 I usually drink tea for breakfast.
2 home / cooks / she / dinner / at / frequently
 ________.
3 in / hungry / morning / the / he / is / always
 ________.
4 breakfast / eat / we / never
 ________.
5 don't / pizza / usually / they / have
 ________.
6 for / are / never / we / work / late
 ________.

➤ Go back to page 37.

Grammar Hub

6.1

there is / there are

	Singular	Plural
Positive	**There is** a bus stop. **There's** a bus stop.	**There are** a lot of boats.
Negative	**There isn't** an airport.	**There aren't** any buses.

- We use *there is/isn't* or *there are/aren't* to say that something exists (or doesn't exist). We can use *there is / there are* to describe different places or things in a house, town, etc.

  There are a lot of flowers in the yard.
  There's a bookstore in the center of town.
- We use *there is* with a singular noun and *there are* with a plural noun.

  There's a bank in the city center.
  There are bus stops on this street.
- We use *some* and *a lot of* with plural nouns in positive sentences.

  There are some nice cafés in my neighborhood.
  There are a lot of hotels in this city.
- We use *any* and *a lot of* with plural nouns in negative sentences.

  There aren't any museums in my town.
  There aren't a lot of tourists here.

	some / a lot of / any
Positive	There are **some** big buildings.
	There are **a lot of** museums.
Negative	There aren't **any** islands.
	There aren't **a lot of** stores.

Be careful!

- In sentences with more than one noun, the verb agrees with the first noun.

  There's a hotel and a grocery store.
  There are ten stores and a large hotel.
  There's a park and two swimming pools.

6.2

***is there / are there* question forms**

	Question	Positive short answer	Negative short answer
Singular	**Is there** a dresser?	**Yes, there is.**	**No, there isn't.**
Plural	**Are there** cushions?	**Yes, there are.**	**No, there aren't.**

	Question
a lot of	Are there **a lot of** books?
any	Are there **any** chairs?

- We use *Is there …?* or *Are there …?* to ask about different places and objects.

  Is there a library in town?
  Are there cushions on the couch?
- We use *Is there …?* with a singular noun and *Are there …?* with a plural noun.

  Is there a bathtub in the bathroom?
  Are there pictures on the wall?
- We can use *a lot of* and *any* in questions about plural nouns.

  Are there a lot of books on the bookshelf?
  Are there any cups in the kitchen?

Be careful!

- We use *there is* not *there's* in a positive short answer.

  Yes, there is. NOT ~~*Yes, there's.*~~

6.1

There is / There are

A Choose the correct options to complete the sentences.

1 There aren't *some* / *any* cars in Venice.
2 There are *a lot of* / *any* water taxis.
3 There *'s* / *are* 350 boats (called 'gondolas') in Venice.
4 There are about 400 boatmen but there *'s* / *are* only one woman!
5 There are *a* / *some* narrow streets in Venice. One street is only 53 centimeters wide!
6 There are *some* / *any* very old buildings in Venice – the Palazzo Grimani Museum is more than 500 years old!

B Complete the description with *there is/there isn't* or *there are/aren't*.

I live in a small town and [1] ___there aren't___ a lot of restaurants. [2] ________ one small café where you can get tea and coffee or juice. [3] ________ a lot of things to do in my town – it's very boring really – but [4] ________ a nice park. I usually play soccer there with my friends on Saturdays. It's a very small place, so [5] ________ any art galleries and [6] ________ a museum. You have to go to the city to find those, but [7] ________ two small stores. [8] ________ a train station and that's very important for me and my friends because we get the train into the city. In the city, [9] ________ a big shopping mall and we go there to buy clothes.

C Complete the sentences with the correct form of the noun in parentheses. Add *a* or *an* if necessary.

1 There are a lot of ___flowers___ (*flower*) in our yard.
2 There's a TV and ___a computer___ (*computer*).
3 There aren't any ________ (*book*) on the bookshelf.
4 There are ten ________ (*chair*) and a big table.
5 There's ________ (*fridge*) in the kitchen.
6 There isn't ________ (*apple tree*) in the backyard.
7 There aren't a lot of ________ (*plant*) on the balcony.
8 There are some ________ (*cushion*) on the floor.

➤ Go back to page 43.

6.2

***Is there / Are there* question forms**

A Complete the questions with *Is* or *Are*.

1 ___Is___ there a bookcase in your bedroom?
2 ________ there a big window?
3 ________ there two beds in your bedroom?
4 ________ there a lot of cushions on your couch?
5 ________ there any photos on the walls?
6 ________ there a TV in your bedroom?
7 ________ there a desk by the window?
8 ________ there a lot of things under your bed?

B Answer the questions in Exercise A.

1 Yes, there ___is___.
2 No, there ________.
3 Yes, there ________.
4 No, there ________.
5 Yes, there ________.
6 No, there ________.
7 Yes, there ________.
8 No, there ________.

C Use the prompts to create questions using *Is there* and *Are there*.

1 a lot of / cabinets / kitchen
________?
2 a lamp / desk
________?
3 any / books / bookshelf
________?
4 clock / wall
________?
5 cups / coffee table
________?
6 any / mirrors / bathroom
________?
7 blue cushions / couch
________?
8 rug / bedroom floor
________?

➤ Go back to page 45

Vocabulary Hub

1.2 Jobs

Match the words in the box with the pictures.

an actor   a builder   a chef   a musician   a photographer   a police officer   a receptionist   a sales person   a soccer player   a writer

1 ______

2 ______

3 ______

4 ______

5 ______

6 ______

7 ______

8 ______

9 ______

10 ______

➤ Go back to page 4.

2.1 Nationalities

Look at the flags. Use *-an*, *-ian*, *-ese* or *-ish* to write the nationality for each country.

Algeria

______

Chile

______

Denmark

______

Italy

______

Lebanon

______

Morocco

______

Russia

______

Scotland

______

Venezuela

______

Vietnam

______

➤ Go back to page 10.

2.2 Numbers 11–100

Write these words in numbers.

a thirty-seven *37*
b ninety-two ______
c twenty-four ______
d fifty-one ______
e eighty-three ______
f sixty-five ______
g forty-six ______
h seventy-nine ______

➤ Go back to page 12.

3.1 Objects and colors

Match the words with the colors.

black blue brown green gray red white yellow

a ______ b ______ c ______ d ______ e ______ f ______ g ______ h ______

➤ Go back to page 18.

4.1 Daily activities

Look at the pictures and complete the phrases with the verbs in the box.

go (x2) have read talk watch

1 ______ breakfast

2 ______ home

3 ______ to bed

4 ______ TV / a movie

5 ______ to my friends/family

6 ______ a book

➤ Go back to page 26.

5.2 Food and meals

A Look at the pictures. Practice the words with a partner.

1 ______________

banana

pear

orange

grapes

2 ______________

tomato

broccoli

cucumber

onion

3 ______________

tea

milk

juice

water

4 ______________

chocolate

chips

peanuts

cookies

B Label the food groups.

drinks fruits snacks vegetables

C Add two more words to each group. Tell the class.

➤ Go back to page 36.

6.2 Furniture and rooms

A Look at the picture. Write the correct word next to each number.

coffee table couch fridge
mirror oven rug shower toilet

1 ______________ 5 ______________
2 ______________ 6 ______________
3 ______________ 7 ______________
4 ______________ 8 ______________

B Label the rooms (a–c) with the words in the box.

bathroom kitchen living room

➤ Go back to page 44.

Communication Hub

6.2

Student A

Look at your picture. Your partner has a similar picture but there are eight differences. Ask questions to find the differences.

A: Is there a bed in your picture?

B: Yes, there is.

➤ Go back to page 44.

1.2

Student B

A PLAN Imagine this woman is your friend. Complete the information about her with your own ideas.

First name ______________________

Last name ______________________

Country ______________________

City ______________________

Job ______________________

B PREPARE Prepare to introduce your friend to your partner. Practice by yourself.

This is a picture of my friend. Her name is Cristina. She's from …

C PRACTICE Work in pairs. Listen to your partner's introduction.

D REPEAT Introduce your friend to your partner.

➤ Go back to page 5.

4.2

Student B

A PREPARE Look at the picture. Write questions to find the missing information.

1 what / called ______________________________?
2 where / live ______________________________?
3 where / go / in the fall ______________________________?
4 where / go / in the spring ______________________________?
5 how far / go *How far do they go every year*?

B DISCUSS Ask your partner the questions in Exercise A. Complete the missing information.

C DISCUSS Read the information about Arctic terns. Answer your partner's questions.

Name: Arctic terns
Where: The Arctic and the Antarctic
When: In August or September they go to the Antarctic. In May or June they go to the Arctic.
How far: About 44,000 miles per year (70,800 kilometers)

➤ Go back to page 29.

2.2

Student B

A PREPARE Read the information. What questions can you ask to find the missing information?

Write your questions here.

1 *Where's Victor Moretti from?* ?

2 ____________________?

3 ____________________?

4 ____________________?

5 ____________________?

6 ____________________?

7 ____________________?

8 ____________________?

B PRACTICE Ask your partner questions to complete the information about each person.

a

Name	Victor Moretti
Country	1 ______
Age	28
Job	2 ______

b

Name	3 ______
Country	Japan
Age	4 ______
Job	Doctor

c

Name	Dev Gupta
Country	5 ______
Age	42
Job	6 ______

d

Name	Zehra Yilmaz
Country	7 ______
Age	8 ______
Job	Computer programmer

➤ Go back to page 13.

6.2

Student B

Look at your picture. Your partner has a similar picture but there are eight differences. Ask questions to find the differences.

A: Is there a bed in your picture?

B: Yes, there is.

➤ Go back to page 44.

Communication Hub

6.2

Student B

A PREPARE You want to rent a room from your partner. Read the description of what you need. Write five questions to ask your partner.

- a table. *Is there a table?*
- lamps.
- a large window.
- the internet.
- near museums and theaters.
- near restaurants.

B SPEAK Answer your partner's questions. Use the information in the advertisement.

Your room:

- Comfortable room in quiet area.
- 10 minutes from train station.
- Near stores and restaurants.
- Has a bed, desk, chair and lamp.

$250 per week.

C REPEAT Ask your partner questions about their room. Find out if it is the right place for you.

A: Can I ask about the room for rent?
B: Yes, of course. How can I help you?
A: Is it near museums and theaters?
B: Yes, it is.

D REPORT Tell the class about the room.

I like / don't like my partner's room because …

➤ Go back to page 45.

3.1

Coatroom attendant

Turn your back, or leave the room, for two minutes.

You are a coatroom attendant. The others are customers.

Look for their objects and check that you have the correct things. Ask about:

1 the name of the object/objects (hat, bag, headphones, etc)

2 the color/colors (red, blue, black and white, gray and brown)

Remember: *this/these*.

Change roles and repeat.

Are these your glasses?

➤ Go back to page 19.

Irregular Verbs

Base form	Simple past	Past participle
be	was/were	been
become	became	become
begin	began	begun
break	broke	broken
bring	brought	brought
build	built	built
buy	bought	bought
can	could	(been able to)
catch	caught	caught
choose	chose	chosen
come	came	come
cost	cost	cost
cut	cut	cut
do	did	done
drink	drank	drunk
eat	ate	eaten
fall	fell	fallen
feel	felt	felt
find	found	found
forget	forgot	forgotten
get	got	got
give	gave	given
go	went	gone/been
grow	grew	grown
have	had	had
hear	heard	heard
hit	hit	hit
hold	held	held
hurt	hurt	hurt
keep	kept	kept
know	knew	known
leave	left	left
lend	lent	lent

Base form	Simple past	Past participle
let	let	let
lose	lost	lost
make	made	made
mean	meant	meant
meet	met	met
must	had to	(had to)
pay	paid	paid
put	put	put
read	read	read
ride	rode	ridden
run	ran	run
say	said	said
see	saw	seen
sell	sold	sold
set	set	set
shut	shut	shut
sing	sang	sung
sit	sat	sat
sleep	slept	slept
speak	spoke	spoken
spell	spelled	spelled
spend	spent	spent
stand	stood	stood
steal	stole	stolen
take	took	taken
teach	taught	taught
tell	told	told
think	thought	thought
throw	threw	thrown
understand	understood	understood
wear	wore	worn
win	won	won
write	wrote	written

PHONETIC SYMBOLS											
Single vowels			Diphthongs			Consonants					
/ɪ/	fish	/fɪʃ/	/uw/	new	/nuw/	/p/	pen	/pen/	/s/	snake	/sneɪk/
/iː/	bean	/biːn/	/eɪ/	face	/feɪs/	/b/	bag	/bæg/	/z/	zoo	/zuː/
/ʊ/	foot	/fʊt/	/ɔɪ/	boy	/bɔɪ/	/t/	tea	/tiː/	/ʃ/	shop	/ʃɒp/
/uː/	shoe	/ʃuː/	/oʊ/	nose	/noʊz/	/d/	dog	/dɒg/	/ʒ/	television	/ˈtelɪvɪʒən/
/e/	egg	/eg/	/ju/	use	/juz/	/ʧ/	chip	/ʧɪp/	/m/	map	/mæp/
/ə/	mother	/ˈmʌðər/	/aɪ/	eye	/aɪ/	/ʤ/	jazz	/ʤæz/	/n/	name	/neɪm/
/ɜː/	word	/wɜːrd/	/aʊ/	mouth	/maʊθ/	/k/	cake	/keɪk/	/ŋ/	ring	/rɪŋ/
/ɔː/	talk	/tɔːk/				/g/	girl	/gɜːrl/	/h/	house	/haʊs/
/æ/	back	/bæk/				/f/	film	/fɪlm/	/l/	leg	/leg/
/ʌ/	bus	/bʌs/				/v/	verb	/vɜːrb/	/r/	road	/roʊd/
/ɑː/	arm	/ɑːrm/				/θ/	thing	/θɪŋ/	/w/	want	/wɒnt/
/ɒ/	top	/tɒp/				/ð/	these	/ðiːz/	/j/	yes	/jes/

Audio scripts

Welcome

The alphabet, Exercise C
0.5
1 Carlos. C – a – r – l – o – s
2 Hassan. H – a – s – s – a – n
3 Erica. E – r – i – c – a

Unit 1

Lesson 1.1 Listening, Exercise B
1.2 **R = Receptionist L = Lisa**

R: Good morning! Can I help you?
L: Hello! Yes, I'd like some English lessons, please.
R: Of course! What's your name?
L: My first name is Lisa, L – i – s – a, and my last name is Fuentes, F – u – e – n – t – e – s.
R: Thank you. Where are you from?
L: I'm from Spain.
R: Are you from Madrid?
L: No, I'm not. I'm from Bilbao.
R: What's your phone number?
L: 0764 729 3387.
R: OK … Now, let's find a class for you …

Unit 2

Lesson 2.2 Listening, Exercise A
2.6 **P = Pete K = Kara A = Angelo M = Maria L = Leila H = Hana**

Conversation 1
P: Hi, Kara! How are you?
K: Hi, Pete! Fine, thanks.
P: Are you free this evening?
K: No, I'm not. I have my Spanish guitar class this evening.
P: Oh, OK! Who's your teacher?
K: Our teacher is Ms. Sanchez.
P: Really? Where's she from?
K: She's from Argentina.

Conversation 2
A: Hi! Is this classroom 12B?
M: Yes, it is. Are you here for the Arabic class, too?
A: Yes, I am. I'm a new student.
M: Great! What's your name?
A: My name's Angelo!
M: Hello, Angelo. I'm Maria. Nice to meet you.
A: Nice to meet you, too.

Conversation 3
L: Good afternoon! Are you a teacher here, too?
H: Yes, I am! My name's Hana. I'm the yoga teacher.
L: Nice to meet you! My name's Leila. I'm the Arabic class teacher.
H: Nice to meet you! When's your class?
L: Now! Bye!
H: OK, bye!

Unit 3

Lesson 3.1 Listening, Exercise A
3.3 **C = Customer CA = Coatroom attendant**

C: Hello. Can I have my coat, please?
CA: Yes. What's your ticket number?
C: It's 42.
CA: 42, OK … here you are.
C: Sorry, that isn't my coat. That's a red coat. My coat's blue.
CA: Oh, sorry. Uh … Is this your coat?
C: No! My coat is blue. That coat is green.
CA: Oh, yes … Is this your coat?
C: No. My coat is blue! That coat is black.
CA: This one?
C: Yes, that's it.
CA: Here you go.
C: Thank you. And can I have my bags, please?
CA: Bags?
C: Yes, there are two bags. One is green and the other one is white.
CA: Are these your bags?
C: No! Those bags are red and blue. My bags are green and white!
CA: Sorry! Sorry! Are these your bags?
C: Yes!
CA: Here you go.
C: Thank you.

Unit 4

Lesson 4.1 Listening, Exercise B
4.2 **P = Presenter A = Astrid M = Magne**

P: My life … the lighthouse keepers.
A: Hello. My name's Astrid. I'm a lighthouse keeper. I live and work in a lighthouse.
M: Hi. I'm Magne. I'm Astrid's husband. I also live and work in the lighthouse. We work in the same place.
A: But we don't work at the same time. I get up very early – at five o'clock in the morning! I start work at five fifteen, and I finish at one thirty in the afternoon.
M: I don't work in the morning. I start work at one thirty in the afternoon, and I finish work late – at nine forty-five in the evening.
A: I relax and watch TV in the afternoon but I don't watch TV in the evening. I make something to eat and then I go to bed at eight o'clock.
M: I watch TV or read a book in the evening. I go to bed at one o'clock in the morning and I get up late at 11 o'clock in the morning.

Unit 5

Lesson 5.1 Listening, Exercise A
5.2 **I = Interviewer W = Woman M = Man**

I: Hi! Do you have a minute? I'd like to ask you some questions.

W: OK. What's it about?

I: It's about how you relax in your free time.

W: OK!

M: Sure!

I: Thanks! Do you work near here?

W: Yes, we both work in the offices over there.

I: Great! Question one: what do you do on your lunch break?

M: Um … I have lunch at my desk; I don't have time to take a break.

W: Yes, he works all the time! He doesn't even take coffee breaks!

I: Do you go to the gym on your lunch break?

W: No, I don't. My friend has a gym at her office and she goes there on her lunch break.

I: That sounds good. Does she go to the gym every day?

W: No, she doesn't. She goes about twice a week.

I: OK. The next question is: what do you do to relax after work?

W: I usually go home and cook a meal, and watch TV.

M: Yeah, I go running after work. After that, I go home and take a bath.

I: OK. Question three: what do you do to relax on the weekend?

W: Umm … well … I go running …

M: Yeah, she goes running and I go food shopping. She doesn't like food shopping!

W: Then I relax in the evening. I cook a nice meal and watch a movie on TV.

I: That's great. Thanks for your time today. Please take a free one-day pass to our new gym!

W: Ooh! Thanks …!

M: Thank you …!

Unit 6

Lesson 6.2 Vocabulary, Exercise B
6.4 **M = Martin**

M: Hi everyone, my name's Martin and I'm looking for someone to rent my room. As you can see, there's a desk and two chairs. There's a big closet. You can put your clothes in there. There's a bookshelf. All my books are on it right now. There's a small table with a lamp on it next to the bed. Oops, my clock is under the bed. Sorry about that! Those are a couple of my pictures on the wall. And there's a window with a nice view of the yard. All this for 200 dollars a month!

Lesson 6.2 Listening, Exercise C
6.5 **R = Realtor M = Man**

R: Hi! This is New York City Rentals. How can I help you?

M: Hello. I'd like some information about the studio for rent on East 23rd Street.

R: Sure! No problem. Let's see. That's number 25B, the studio? What would you like to know?

M: Are there any buses on that street?

R: Yes, there are. It's about a 10-minute walk to the bus stop.

M: OK. Are there any stores nearby?

R: Yes, there are. There's a grocery store on the corner and there are a lot of restaurants nearby.

M: Is there a living room and a bedroom?

R: No, it's a studio. There's only one room.

M: Oh, I see. What about the furniture? What's in the room? Are there any chairs?

R: No, there aren't. There are some bookshelves, a lamp and a bed. That's all. It's a small studio …

M: There's no desk and no chair. Hmm. Is there a large window?

R: Yes, there's a large window with a view of the park.

M: Is there a bathroom?

R: Yes, there is. There's a small bathroom with a shower, but no bathtub.

M: Is there a kitchen?

R: No, there isn't. It's just one room!

M: No kitchen and no bathtub, and you want $2,000 a month! You must be joking!

Notes

Macmillan Education Limited
4 Crinan Street
London N1 9XW

Companies and representatives throughout the world

American Language Hub Starter A Student's Book ISBN 978-1-380-04676-5
American Language Hub Starter A Student's Book with Student's App
ISBN 978-1-380-04670-3

Written by Ingrid Wisniewska and Ed Price

First published 2020

Designed by emc design ltd
Illustrated by Daniel Límon (Beehive Illustration) ppvi, 18, 19, 20, 23, 24, 42, 44, 46, 47, 48, XI, XVIII, XXI.
Cover design by Restless
Cover photograph by Getty Images/Valentinrussanov
Picture research by Emily Taylor
Café Hub videos produced by Creative Listening.
Café Hub video scripts written by James and Luke Vyner.

Authors' acknowledgements
Ingrid Wisniewska would like to thank her husband Greg for his constant support and encouragement.

Ed Price would like to give special thanks, always, to Becca and Henry.

The authors and publishers would like to thank the following for permission to reproduce their photographs:

Alamy pp32, 36(i,l), Galyna Andrushko p29a, Blickwinkel p29(tr), Piero Cruciatti p10(tl), Bella Falk p2(bl), Galopin p29(d), Jiri Hubatka p20(2), John Warburton-Lee Photography p36(Sara), Alex Robinson p10(2), Viktorus p40(3), Westend61 p34(2), Jan Wlodarczyk p26(tr); **BrandX** pp24(tl), 45, XX(pear); **Caiaimage**/Great Images p20(3); **Getty Images** pp2(tr), 4(8), 6(4,7,8), 34(7), 34(8), 36(buffet), XIX(4,5,6), XX(orange, broccoli, milk, water, nuts), AFP p10(tml), Age fotostock p42, Ursula Alter p40(2), Ben Pipe Photography p34(br), Michael Blann p23(cr), Blend Images/Chris Clor p34(4), Blend Images/Jeremy Woodhouse/Holly Wilmeth p9, Blue Jean Images pXVIII(3), Nick Brundle p2(tl), Gary Burchell p34(3), Caiaimage p26(d), Caiaimage/Tom Merton p7(br), Caiaimage/Chris Ryan p4(5), Corbis/Robbie Jack p10(1), Cultura RF p36(Davide), Nick David p4(b), Peter Dazeley p6(6), Steve Debenport p12(2), Den-belitsky pp38–39(background), Dan Dunkley pXVIII(1), E+ pp40(1), XVIII(6), XIX(2), EyeEm pp2(bl), 6(3), 30–31(background), 25, EyeEm/Zuzana Gajdosikova p40(4), Fcafotodigital p36(c, tr), First Light pp20(tl), XVIII(10), Flashpop pp13(b), XXIII(b), David Freund pXXI, Tony Garcia pXIX(1), Hadynyah pp28–29, Hero Images pp3, 4(6,7), 15(bl), 34(bl), Nicolas Herrbach p4(1), Timothy Hiatt p10(tmr), The Image Bank pp27, 33, 34(6), Image Source p5, iStockphoto pp26(c), 28(a–d), 29(b), 36(e,j), XX(chips, cookies), Gavriel Jecan pXXII, Jetta Productions Inc pp13(c), XXIII(c), John Lamb pXVIII(4), Lee Pei Ling pp6–7(background), Lonely Planet Images p43(tr), Peter Lourenco p21, MackoFlower p36(tmr), David Madison pp22–23(background), Maskot pp13(a), 12(1), XXIII(a), Simon McGill p30(takeaway cup), Mint Images p6(1), Abel Mitja Varela p20(4), Moment RF pp29(c), 40(cm), Monkeybusinessimages p26(b), Tara Moore p26(a), Aleksandar Nakic p4(2), Jekaterina Nikitina p20(1), Gary John Norman pXIX(3), Steve Outram p6(2), PhotoDisc p36(g), Photolibrary pp36(tm), 43(bl), Photographer's Choice p36(k), Steve Prezant p15(br), Robert Harding World Imagery p1, Marc Romanelli p12(3), RooM RF pp40(5), Sergione Infuso p11, Shironosov pvi, Robin Skjoldborg pp13(d), XXIII(d), SolisImages p4(3), SolStock p48, Tetra images pp6(5), XVIII(7), Thomas M. Barwick INC p34(5), Todor Tsvetkov p24(tr), Bernd Vogel pXVIII(9), Art Wager pp46–47(background), Westend61 pp4(4), 34(1); **Hill Street Studios** pXVIII(8); **Lisa Payne Photography** pXX(juice); **iStockphoto** pp35, 36(h,d,f), 37(Natalia), XVIII(2); **Macmillan Education Ltd** ppXVIII(Russia), XX(tea), Paul Bricknell pp36(a), XX(banana, grapes); **Microzoa** p36(b); **PlainPicture**/Elektrons 08 p17, Jason Langley photography p41; **Scheifoto**/Espen Gresvik Schei p10(tr); **Shutterstock**/Watcharapong Saiboot pp14–15(background); **Superstock** pXVIII(all flags ex Russia); **Thinkstock** pp30(cup&saucer), 40(6), XVIII(5), XX(onion, chocolate); **Up the Resolution** pXX(tomato, cucumber).

Commissioned photographs by Creative Listening pp6, 7, 14, 15, 22, 23, 30, 31, 38, 39, 46 and 47.

Printed and bound in Brazil

2025

8